CORPORATE
Nirvana

A Fable of Urban Enlightenment

Sonali Masih-D'silva

CORPORATE Nirvana

A Fable of Urban Enlightenment

Sonali Masih-D'silva

EBD

EMBASSY BOOKS
www.embassybooks.in

CORPORATE
Nirvana

A Fable of Urban Enlightenment

© Sonali Masih-D'silva
First Published in India: 2011

Published by:
EMBASSY BOOK DISTRIBUTORS
120, Great Western Building,
Maharashtra Chamber of Commerce Lane,
Fort, Mumbai-400 023, (India)
Tel : (+91-22) 22819546 / 32967415
email : embassy@vsnl.com
Website: www.embassybooks.in

ISBN 13: 978-93-80227-85-6

Dedication

To my father for being my first teacher

Acknowledgements

This book is a joint effort in the true sense. Corporate Nirvana would have been impossible without the unstinted support of family, friends, and colleagues, who helped me finish what I started.

I am deeply thankful to my late father, Dr. Sohan Masih, who taught me the value of reading and writing, amongst many other things. I owe a heartfelt thanks to my spirited mother, Roseline Melville-Masih, who is an excellent example of living in the moment.

I owe a very special thanks to my husband, Manohar, for his unconditional love and support. He has been part of every stage of this book. I thank him for being there, no matter what, and for reminding me that I must pursue my passion in life.

A big thanks to my elder sister, Sapna, for her wisdom and abundant love. She's been my friend, (third) parent, and sister, all rolled into one. I must say thanks to my brother-in-law, Nalin, who has been very generous and encouraging all through. I genuinely admire my little niece, Sana, whose ultimate goal in life is to be happy. I am very grateful that I have parents-in-law, and a second family, who love and support me as much as they do. Preethy, my best friend, has been a pillar of strength for many years now, and I am indebted to her for her genuine love and honest advice.

I wish to thank all my wonderful friends and well-wishers who cheered me on to complete this project. At times, help and affection comes from the most unexpected people and situations. I consider it a privilege that so many people have touched my life and brought me this far.

A sincere acknowledgement is due to my publisher. I am immensely grateful to Sohin Lakhani of Embassy Books, for agreeing to publish my book. I admire him for not just being a great colleague, but for his warmth, friendship, and good advice. This was fun! I have a special note of thanks for Varsha Shah of Embassy Books, who through her professionalism and insight, made my job so much easier. I genuinely appreciate Swati Chopra for editing the book and Sandesh for designing a great cover. A big thank you is due to Divya Dubey of Gyaana Books for her support all through.

And if you have picked up this book to read, I thank you from the bottom of my heart.

Sonali Masih-D'silva

July, 2011

Introduction

I had never given much thought to how a book is written until I wrote one myself. Around April 2010, on a hot and humid day in Delhi, I was contemplating how life had brought me full circle. One thought led to another, and I had already completed the first chapter by midnight the same day. Corporate Nirvana is full of principles and ideas that I deeply believe in. These have worked wonders in my own life.

In the book, I often speak about the power of the Universe. I use the word 'Universe' as a symbol of universal power. Feel free to substitute the word with your own spiritual belief, if that helps you while reading. The reason I mention it is because I have experienced there are unseen forces to help us accomplish goals that seem impossible or too difficult at first. The key lies in believing in ourselves, not in trying too hard. More importantly, we need to know the what beyond a shadow of doubt or indecision. I also call this our ultimate goal. The how, and when, and where gets worked out. The universal power then comes into being right away.

I knew deep down that I wanted to write a book about personal leadership. I had no idea who might publish it or if it would turn out to be a success. I chose not to think too hard about the outcome of it. If I did, I know this book would not be in your hands right now. Even though I had no contacts in the publishing industry, I did have an insane amount of belief that this book would reach a bookstore soon. Did all of this happen without planning? Not really. I did plan to pick up the phone and call a publisher (the only one I did, after looking them up on the internet). At the same time, I never planned it to conclude exactly this way. I have observed that life takes its own course. We must help things along by believing and enjoying what we are doing.

This is not my original thought, and I lay no claim to it. Spiritual literature dating back thousands of years speaks of the same power. Though, I did not read ancient texts to discover this principle of personal power. I unwittingly experienced the principle ten years ago, and realised that it exists and works for us. I only take credit for the story and the context it is set in.

I want to share with you that I have tried my best to make the characters of my book credible, and part of everyday life. I am a great fan of the uncommon power of the common person. I have met many people who are incredibly wise and intelligent, while they live a busy and urban life. These include retired people, executives, homemakers, teenagers, and even village folk. These ordinary people stun me with their insight and good judgement. Therefore, I consider them extraordinary. I find this path to wisdom more likely than bumping into a mystical robe clad person far removed from our reality. Which is why, this is a fable of urban enlightenment.

The book is arranged in nine chapters. Each chapter begins with the most important lessons of that chapter. Each of the nine ends with a summary page that captures its essence and practical strategies. My idea is to help you to absorb what you read. You will find two useful worksheets at the back of the book to help explore your personal power. I genuinely hope that these tools will enable you to answer some of your life's questions, and move to greater success and happiness.

To your best,

Sonali Masih-D'silva

"Set a goal to achieve something that is so big, so exhilarating that it excites you and scares you at the same time. It must be a goal that is so appealing, so much in line with your spiritual core that you can't get it out of your mind. If you do not get chills when you set a goal, you're not setting big enough goals."

Bob Proctor

For YOU !

When your soul turns weary in your quest for success, may you find the greatest triumph waiting at your doorstep.

If you feel defeated, let your life shine upon others, for they may need it more than you.

And when life throws a stone at you, may your touch transform it into a beautiful rose.

As you take on this world to prove your worth, may you first prove worthy to yourself.

I pray you have the wisdom to create love in your home, and not just love the four walls of your home.

Let all material possessions be yours, if you wish, but that you do not turn into a possession yourself.

In your darkest hour, may you feel the invisible strength of faith, and the Universe become your beacon as you seek your chosen path.

When you hope and pray for just one door to open, let abundance open many for you.

Life might withhold some answers, but may they all come to you when you ask the right questions.

I wish for you abundant wealth, true joy, radiant health, and timeless wisdom.

May it be as easy for you as it was for me.

This is my wish for you.

Contents

CHAPTER **PAGE**

1. A Personal Breakthrough   3

2. A Ray of Hope   15

3. The Guru Speaks   29

4. An Unlikely Teacher   45

5. Path to a Fulfilling Life   59

6. Meeting a Secret Stranger   71

7. A Family Reunited   87

8. Message in the Mountains   99

9. An Awakened Life   119

Lessons of Chapter One

Why live a mediocre life when you can live a superlative one

Ordinary people have the absolute potential to become extraordinary

Life has plans for us that are more magnificent than what our limited imagination can conceive of

It is not the privilege of a chosen few to be enlightened, we are all enlightened

CHAPTER 1

A Personal Breakthrough

"More than anything else, I believe it's our decisions, not the conditions of our lives that determine our destiny."

~**Anthony Robbins**

What I am about to sharewith you might surprise you greatly. It surprised me, I can tell you that. In fact, you might even disbelieve me for a while. After all, how often do you find real people who have experienced true transformation in just a few months! I wasted years of my life thinking I was living a life that was almost impossible to step out of. The moment I walked away from it, I realised how easy it is. To tell you the truth, I am just an everyday kind of person deep down, so what is possible for me could be so for you too. I know I am putting myself on the line here, but I am going to say something important to you. The simple but profound lessons that you will discover in the next nine chapters really work, because they are based on certain principles. I assure you that stunning results will follow if you put in practice what you are about to learn.

To succeed like this, way beyond your imagination, and still have a balanced life, is more achievable than you think. We can be successful *and* happy. We can have lots of money *and* be at peace. We can be busy *and* spare time for our interests. We can work hard *and* have great relationships. These are not paradoxes. We just need to know how to get there in, one step at a time. And this book will do exactly that. Personal transformation is far simpler than we make it out to be. You can actually plan your breakthrough at your own pace, and include all the key lessons you read about in this book. Though, I must add, the sooner, the better. Why live a mediocre life when you can live a superlative one!

Like all worthwhile pursuits in life, these wise lessons will demand your time, attention, and effort. I feel a sense of excitement as I embark on this exhilarating story with you. Every time I revisit these gems, I find new ways to reinvent our life. Knowledge has the greatest impact when shared. My role all through is to humbly put forth what I have learnt from Masters, no less. I take no credit for these profound teachings. My job is to let you decide for yourself if you find them useful.

The best part is that these priceless nuggets of wisdom are universally applicable to each and every one of us. No exceptions. You are meant to succeed beyond your wildest dreams. It does not matter if you are ridden with guilt, or in the depths of despair, or barely able to make ends meet, have no support from people you love, and can't see a way out right now. Forgive me for saying so, but these are mere excuses, however true they might appear to be. Unsuccessful people use these excuses to hide their lack of initiative. Actually, your destiny is in your hands. You create your world, one way or the other. So, feel free to include yourself in that list of people who are meant to succeed spectacularly. If you ever thought you weren't cut out to be there then banish such thoughts. Like I said, we all qualify!

There is a good reason why I say this so confidently. I trust with all my heart that there exists a deep desire in each of us to attain greatness, to be something more than just an average person – to be the best version of ourselves that we can possibly be. Under the layers of daily pressures and their tiring grind, is a limitless potential to live our best. I know with absolute conviction that you can be your best, live your best, and enjoy your best. You have an ability to excel – to be better than what you were yesterday.

Here is an important thought - what is believable is achievable. That is worth pausing and thinking about. Here's another one, and it may sound profound to you, but is simply the truth: 'Ordinary people have the absolute potential to become extraordinary.' Simple, but powerful, as one of my teachers said. Every one of us has the potential to live a supremely happy and fulfilling life. I've experienced life at its worst, and found extraordinarily powerful insights to turn things around.

I've come to understand that the Universe has plans for us that are more magnificent than what our limited imagination can conceive of. Imagine, powerful forces work for you every moment to help you become successful! That is really something. I might never have discovered this wisdom but for some amazing people I met. Those exciting meetings happened quite by chance, and the wonderful men and women I met, opened doors that I never knew existed. The best part is, you don't have to go looking for these people. My job is to crystallise their life-changing lessons right here, within the two covers of this book. As I introduce you to these teachers one-by-one, I hope you will find inspiration, joy, learning, and immense happiness. Believe me, I did. I am still an ordinary human being, but my story isn't.

Before I begin, I must share how it all began. I owe you that much. Maybe, you will find some of your own self in my story. Like several of us I came from wretched beginnings. Soon, I was tired of having less and wanting more. Of seeing others have what I thought I deserved as well. I am not sure if there is an ideal amount of money or success that ensures enduring satisfaction. After having achieved which we can sit back and enjoy life. The success trap is a vicious cycle – I know this because I was caught in it for several years. Sounds familiar? I don't deny that we all need to work hard on our careers. But there is a thin line of difference between working hard and slogging.

I thought I had good reason to slog in life. I belonged to a poor family. Even though we lacked money, my parents taught me the value of honesty, respect, and hard work above all else. Over the years, I lost my parents one by one to prolonged illnesses. For years, I drowned in my guilt, wondering if I could have saved them if I had been a successful and wealthy son. I guess that thought propelled me to work like a mad man.

Along the way, I found Nina, the love of my life. We got married, and I worked harder still to give my family all that I couldn't give my parents. Weeks turned into months, and months into years. My career soared. I ate, breathed, and drank my work. Addiction and dedication are not that far apart. I had lost my perspective long ago. After twenty-five years of giving my sweat and blood, I became CEO of one of India's top three IT companies. Finally, I felt I had become a man of consequence. In my greed for success and power, I never noticed that my family was drifting away from me. Nina and our two beautiful children, Anya and Neil, had practically given up on me, I guess.

I am not sure why most of us don't see a downward spiral in our lives until it is too late. One day, I had a heart attack and was rushed to the hospital. There was little hope of my survival. Lying in that hospital bed made me realise the value of what I had disrespected. I knew in my heart that I needed a second chance to set our life right. In that instant, something tremendous happened for both Nina and I. We forgave each other for all the hurts of the past. Love is the only power we have when we feel powerless. I am not sure if what I felt was mystical, spiritual or philosophical. Call it what you wish, but I felt unimaginable joy. A brilliant, shining light spread all around me, and at the risk of sounding delirious, I felt a spiritual shift had happened for both of us. Life took on a wonderful new meaning, and has never been the same since then!

That day was truly the beginning of my awakened life, and the magic began unfolding effortlessly. One secret of living a fulfilling life flowed into another, and another. Very soon, the jigsaw fell into place, and a life I never thought existed, began to reveal itself to me. I went on a personal journey and received some stunning insights.

Someone wise once said that without adversity and hardships, our life might just be a series of mediocre attempts. I couldn't agree more. Pain is a great teacher. After being beaten down in life, I found great learning. We don't need to be a genius to reap the benefits of these magnificent but simple lessons. I am certainly not one. In fact, I've spent most of my life trying to appear smarter than I really am. Thankfully, now there is no need to take that hard route to success.

It is not the privilege of a chosen few to be enlightened, we are all enlightened. Changing the landscape of our life is not easy; but it is staggeringly simple. It all starts with the person in the mirror – You! You can be your own guru, guiding yourself to the best you can be. All of this can come true in your life, if only you have faith and conviction. I can't wait to share how all this became possible for me. Let me jump headlong into an ordinary day that turned into a memorable one.

CHAPTER 1

A Personal Breakthrough

Quotable Quote: Why live a mediocre life when you can live a superlative one

5 Powerful Thoughts

➤ Ordinary people have the potential to become extraordinary

➤ The Universe has magnificent plans for us, we can be superbly successful, if we believe in ourselves

➤ We are all enlightened, we all have innate wisdom to be our best

➤ Our destiny is in our hands, we are the master craftsman of our future

➤ Excelling everyday in a small way makes us succeed in a big way in our future

The Master Key: Tap into your inner desire to be your best, live your best, and enjoy your best

Action Point

Put down your strengths on paper and stick them where you can see them every day. Make a list of your limitations, then shift your focus away from them. You need only your strengths to succeed.

LESSONS OF CHAPTER TWO

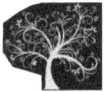

When we listen to our heart, life immediately becomes better

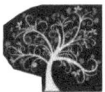

Judging others by appearances stops us from seeing their true value

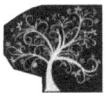

Life is more than running around, it is also about stopping once in a while

Think a thought long enough, and it will come true

CHAPTER 2

A Ray of Hope

"Man often becomes what he believes himself to be. If I keep on saying to myself that I cannot do a certain thing, it is possible that I may end by really becoming incapable of doing it. On the contrary, if I shall have the belief that I can do it, I shall surely acquire the capacity to do it, even if I may not have it at the beginning."

~**Mahatma Gandhi**

What we believe deeply appears in our physical reality. What we have faith about comes about. Unexpected outcomes are the natural consequences of a deep faith. My faith had deepened, and I knew a better life awaited us. How and when, I did not know, but I was sure that my life was no longer the same. My mind was going to places I had not allowed it to explore before. Life began to change in seemingly insignificant ways.

One day, as I stepped out of the car outside my home, I saw a really old woman trying to cross the road over to our side. Seeing no one else around, I helped her cross over. She looked up at me, and there was startling clarity in her deep black eyes set in her wrinkled face; they sparkled with liveliness such that I hadn't seen even in young people. At least not in any of my team members, I thought with some amusement. She surprised me a second time with her deep and robust voice. "Thanks a lot for that. I just hurt my leg, and was walking slowly. We need more people like you who would stop to help." She looked at me so keenly that I felt uncomfortable. I let go her arm in some embarrassment. I had never been good around women, and generally avoided conversation to save myself from precisely such situations. "Would you like to come in for a cup of tea?" She asked cheerfully, breaking my train of thought. "Thanks a lot, but I must get home now. My wife is waiting for me," I mumbled as I took a few steps back.

"So, get her, too," she added helpfully, taking a few steps towards me. "That way I get to meet both of you together. Actually, I am your new next-door neighbour. I did see you in the morning, but you were in a hurry. By the way, I am Maya," she said with a bright smile. Great, that's all we needed, I thought. A nosey old neighbour that made no bones about spying on us. That day, I could not see her beyond my limited perception. Just in case, you thought I homed in on my first wise teacher right away, nothing as dramatic as that happened. Judging others by appearances stops us from seeing their true value. Maya seemed too chatty and downright annoying to me in that first meeting. I couldn't have been more wrong. I didn't see that our old neighbour was to become one of my first instructors on life, living, and true leadership.

I sighed in resignation and accepted her invitation. In fifteen minutes' time, Nina and I were ringing Maya's doorbell. The door swung open within seconds, and Maya energetically greeted us. She stepped forward and gave Nina a bear hug. Nina looked surprised, and glanced at me. I shrugged as I stepped in, and stopped in my tracks as a riot of colours and textures hit me. Maya's home was bright and beautiful. It was breathtaking in its own quirky, crazy way. All four walls of her living room were painted a different, bright colour. This was one heck of an eccentric colour scheme, I thought to myself, looking around. Maya noticed the look on my face. "Old people do have their favourite colours, you know," she said with a mischievous twinkle in her eye. I flushed with obvious embarrassment, and Nina nudged me. We sank into a comfortable sofa, and Maya went in to get us some hot tea. If for nothing else, this visit was worth the flavourful tea, I thought, as the delicious aroma wafted from the kitchen. My poison was 'tea', as I loved saying.

With Maya in the kitchen, I glanced around curiously. I noticed, there was only one object on each of the four walls.

Nothing else adorned them except the object that stood out. The wall facing me was bright Yellow. A single painting of a brilliantly glowing earthen lamp hung in the centre. There was darkness under the lamp, and a halo of light above it. There was something riveting about the simplicity of the artist's vision. I could almost feel the warmth of the glow.

To the right was a bright Blue wall. A piece of furniture was hanging on it – a beautifully carved oak wood bookshelf. The rich texture of the wood gave the stacked books a regal look. As I peered at the titles I saw religious texts of almost all religions I had heard of. Maya had autobiographies of numerous great men and women, including Mahatma Gandhi's. Someone I admired myself. There were many books on science and quantum physics, spirituality and meditation. I noticed books about nature, farming, and plants as well. Maya seemed eclectic in her choice of books, I thought. I began to wonder if she was just an annoying neighbour or whether I had misjudged her terribly.

With that doubt lingering in my mind I looked to my left, at a bright Red wall. An old, large, black and white family photo hung in the centre. There was no telling who these people were, but it seemed to have been put up with great respect and honour. I turned around, curious to figure out the last wall which was directly behind me. It was bright Green. I was startled to see a single window overlooking Maya's stunning garden. A potted plant on the sill was resplendent with multicoloured flowers. Yellow, Blue, Red, Green. What was this supposed to mean? Was it some kind of practical joke she was playing on her unsuspecting visitors?

Just then Maya entered with a tray of tea and cookies. As I

sat munching on the delicious homemade cookies and sipping the flavourful tea, I tried guessing Maya's age. She definitely looked somewhere around eighty. The only confusing part was that sparkle in her eyes and her steady voice. Sounds absurd, but she had a strange youthfulness about her that puzzled me. I bet I looked my age, I thought with some envy.

"So, do you live all by yourself here?" Nina asked her. "How can I be alone? I have wonderful neighbours here; their families are like my own," Maya answered smiling broadly, and I noticed a twinkle in her bright eyes. Considering her friendliness, I wasn't surprised at this bit of information. Honestly, our social visit hadn't been half as bad as I had imagined. I was more intrigued by Maya and her curious home than I cared to admit. Nina invited her over to our house the next evening to have dinner. I wondered if there was a reason Maya was our neighbour. Well, I would find out soon enough I thought, as we wished her good-night. Meeting Maya that night made me feel happy. I reluctantly admitted to myself that I had truly enjoyed this unexpected evening.

Have you noticed that when we listen to our heart, life immediately becomes better? We feel happy and at peace. I had experienced the reverse of this as well. When I refused to listen to my heart, my life went out of whack. Even easy tasks became painful. I felt depressed and lonely for no reason, and money lost all its charm. Since then, I have discovered that our joy is a magnificent compass that always points in the right direction. Lack of joy is a warning signal that can set us on the right course again. Improving our life and circumstances can be a gradual process, but just the decision to make things better results in instant happiness. There is no time lag between a good decision and improved feelings. Our feelings then guide us to further good actions. Good stuff began to happen as soon as I decided to change my life for the better. On an ordinary day in a most unexpected manner, I had met my first teacher - Maya.

I got back home the next day truly looking forward to having our new neighbour over. Maya was right on time. She wore a beige flowing kurta with matching beige pants. She had a pure white chrysanthemum stuck in her neat bun. Maya almost looked like a saint to me in that moment. I shook myself out of my reverie and we settled down to chat. Little did I know that this casual meeting was about to turn into one of the most interesting ones ever.

"Everything is changing so fast, it's a mad world we live in. Maya, you must know more than us what a different world this is." Nina asked. "Yes, I know what you mean dear; we have so much more money today, but so little time to enjoy it." Maya looked up at me as she announced this. Her statement hit me like a bullet. Nina and I exchanged a startled look. "Why do you say that?" I probed. "Well, you are right in asking that because I am not part of the mainstream of this busy city, but I watch others. Just observing when they leave for office and get back at night is a simple way of figuring that out. If you devote so much time to your work and own an expensive car, you must be earning a good amount of money. But if you are not home then you don't have the time to enjoy it. Life is more than running around, you know, it is also about stopping once in a while," she said casually, and continued to eat. I mulled over this as we finished with dinner.

I decided to ask her one more question that had been on

my mind for a while. "I mean this in a good way, Maya, but you seem really healthy for your age. How do you manage that?" I asked with open curiosity.

"Thanks for the compliment. I don't have any age-related problems. I am blessed to have a healthy mind and body that keeps me young, I guess," she revealed.

The mystery just deepened. This made no sense. Our geriatric neighbour had no age-related illnesses? How could that be? She indeed looked fit as a fiddle, and full of energy and good humour. Heck, I was just forty-nine, and a heart attack had nearly killed me. Maya, seeing our confused expressions, shared a secret. I still hold her advice really close to my heart. Believe it or not, I haven't had any major health problems since then. This was Maya's invaluable mantra. "I learnt from my grandfather that health is a mental reality before it becomes a physical reality. Thoughts are very powerful and create our world. If you think a thought long enough it will come true. We must focus on being happy and not worry about falling sick. Thoughts of healing create health. Negative thoughts attract illness. Eating and drinking healthy is less important than thinking and speaking healthy." Maya winked at us, and with that we had reached the end of our interesting evening.

I walked Maya to her door, and just as I was leaving, I turned back and asked a question that had been burning inside me. "How do you have wisdom about new age problems when you haven't faced them yourself?" What Maya said next is one of the most profound lessons I have learnt in life.

"The wisdom you consider new is actually very old. We might be living in a very different world, but the principles of life never change. They are timeless. You wouldn't stop loving your child just because times have changed, would you? Love is timeless. All wisdom and good judgement is as old as this Universe, and has been available to us through the ages. Sometimes we just get too busy to notice the answers we already have," she said calmly.

I saw a look of deep understanding and compassion in her eyes. Nodding my good-night, I thoughtfully walked back home. The insights I got that evening had an unbelievable impact on me. As the wise Eastern saying goes, when the disciple is ready to learn, the teacher appears.

CHAPTER 2

A Ray of Hope

Quotable Quote: What we have faith about, comes about

5 Powerful Thoughts

➤ What we deeply believe in appears in our physical reality. Thoughts turn into things.

➤ Deep, genuine faith in our abilities results in unexpectedly successful outcomes

➤ Our internal joy is our compass. It tells us if we are thinking positively or not. True joy comes from faith and positivity.

➤ Judging others by appearances hides their true value from us

➤ Principles of effective life never change, they are timeless and always applicable

The Master Key: The key to new age problems lies in age-old wisdom

Action Point

Write down every success you desire in your life within the next one year. Be clear and specific about what you want.
Read your desires with conviction and deep faith.
You can achieve every one of them.

Lessons of Chapter Three

When the vision of our life is beautiful, everything else becomes easy

Love is the most important asset we have

A sincere apology creates a new level of understanding with others

We are at our best when we focus on one goal at a time

When we choose our future over our past we have freed ourselves

CHAPTER 3

The Guru Speaks

*"We learn wisdom from failure much more
than from success. We often discover what will
do, by finding out what will not do; and prob-
ably he who never made a mistake,
never made a discovery."*

~Samuel Smiles

The next morning was somehow different. I didn't have all the answers, but an inexplicable confidence surged through me. I knew deep down I had the power to turn around my life for the better. I had faith that help would come when I needed it the most. I had released my prayer with all my heart, and the Universe was responding to me without a doubt. The Universe had actually been waiting to help me all this time. The simplicity of this act seemed absurd to me. Even a few months ago, I would never have believed this to be true. Eye-opening experiences had forced me to examine my inner self. My best life was yet to be lived. And the answers seemed to be getting closer.

As I was driving back home that day, I knew I had to meet Maya again. She knew something I could learn from. Before my courage deserted me, I was already opening her gate. I found her sitting outside, reading a book. She greeted me with a big hug, and I sat down next to her on the airy porch. Her garden was a riot of colours, and the dusk made it all the more beautiful. I began a bit hesitantly. I couldn't stop thinking how weird it was to be asking her these questions when I had known her all of one day!

My mental debate was interrupted by Maya's crisp, steady voice. "You seem worried about something. Is there anything I can do to help?" I marvelled at her accurate observation. It was now or never. "Well, I can't stop thinking about what you said to me last night, Maya. I've been struggling with my excessively busy schedules for years now. My quest for a balanced life is my top priority right now. I just can't seem to figure out what to do first. There are years of neglect and mistakes. Honestly speaking, I am at a bit of a loss. I know I can get there, but how?" The words all came out in a rush.

"I understand your dilemma. At the same time, only you have the answer to what comes first and what is most important to you. Generally, what bothers me the most is first in my mind. Getting entangled in the nitty-gritty of life hides the big picture. Our goal is to keep visualising the big picture we need to attain, and the smaller parts fall into place. Help arrives, wise counsel reaches us, the right people bump into us, and 'happy coincidences' begin to occur. I am not saying all this happens without any effort, but avenues do open up much easier and faster, when we keep our eyes on the goal. When the vision of our life is beautiful, everything becomes easy. The Universe then conspires to help us way beyond our expectations," Maya explained helpfully.

That was a good thumb rule, I thought to myself. She was absolutely right, my priorities were already clear in my mind. I had been too busy getting overwhelmed to have focussed on them. "I have neglected my most important relationships, Maya. My children have distanced themselves from me, and it almost cost me my relationship with Nina. How can I make up for all the hurt I have caused to those I love the most? Am I condemned to live with this guilt forever? Will my kids ever forgive me?" I took a deep breath and looked at her expectantly, hoping for a magic answer.

Maya listened intently with her head inclined, as if absorbing all that I had said and all that I meant. "Now that you know your priority, what can you do to make up for the time you've lost?" Maya asked. I got a sense that she was leading me somewhere rather than give me an easy answer. I thought about it for some time. "No, there is nothing I can do about it, Maya. I have lost a treasured part of my family life which will never come back." I closed my eyes, and my guilt felt like a heavy rock in my chest.

"I don't think you've lost time as much as you seem to have lost the point," she said with a smile. I looked up at her wondering if she was making fun of me. Before I could protest, Maya said something that puzzled me even more. "Knowledge is Light, Love is Life," she stated serenely. Ignoring my confusion, she suddenly got up and gestured to me to follow her. I quickly got up and walked into the bright living room after her. Maya was standing in front of the Yellow wall and intently watching the glowing lamp. This wasn't going the way I had thought. My answer wasn't in that wall, or was it? Maya was decidedly eccentric, just like her house. I hesitatingly stood next to her and cleared my throat. Maya looked at me and smiled. "What do you see?" She asked the obvious. "A glowing lamp," I said simply. "Is that all you see? Try seeing more this time," she egged me on. I took a deep breath and looked intently at the painting. "Umm.... well....it's hung on a Yellow wall, and I can see bright light above the lamp, but there is darkness underneath it," I said, looking at Maya hopefully.

"Well done. If you look at it and think deeply you will find many other meanings in this simple painting," Maya beamed at me. She then turned to the right and stood in front of the Blue wall with the lovely book-case. I was beginning to enjoy this exercise. I felt like a school-kid being tested by a kindly, but stern teacher. I cleared my throat self-consciously for the second time in five minutes. "I can see you read a lot of different kinds of books, Maya. I really appreciate your deep interest in books," I said tentatively. "Thank you for that. I do love books. They are both my treasure and my pleasure. I am never alone, thanks to them. But, are these only books?"

She caught me off-guard. I looked at the book-case again, and then it struck me what Maya's exercise was all about. "Of course," I said slapping my forehead. "Books are knowledge and knowledge spreads light, it dispels darkness. Knowledge is light," I exclaimed, looking at the Yellow and Blue walls by turns. Maya nodded vigorously and patted my shoulder. "I admire you for cracking this much faster than many others in my home. You are a good student. Books are an ocean of wealth, that's why the colour Blue, to remind us of that treasure we all have. All four walls have a wealth of meaning. In fact, many painful issues of life can be solved within the four elements represented here."

Maya briskly walked across the room. She stood in front of the Red wall, gazing at the black and white family photo with deep affection and love. She smiled almost to herself and then looked at me. This time I knew the answer as I looked at the picture. "I assume this is your family, people you love and cherish. Love begins with family. Without those we love, our life is empty. Love is the most important asset we have. It costs nothing and serves everyone for their entire life. I have learnt that lesson through my own bitter experience, Maya," I said sombrely. Maya nodded with wisdom and understanding. "Yes, I couldn't have put it better. That was beautifully said. Red is the colour of love, of passion, of togetherness. Without love, life is meaningless," Maya concluded with a deep breath.

With that we both walked over to the Green wall that had the front door in one corner and a window in the centre. The beautiful flowers bloomed, and swayed in the gentle breeze. I inhaled the magical fragrance of the garden, and it filled me with life and energy. "I had to stand here to fully understand the meaning of this element, Maya. Nature is

34

life. In nature we rejuvenate, find ourselves again, learn to grow and nurture. Am I right about that?" I asked, turning towards her. Maya was smiling broadly at me as she nodded and chuckled. "I must say, you are proving to be the best student I've ever encountered. I love your way with words. And you are absolutely right. Green is the colour of nature, of life. When we lose touch with our surroundings and our basics, life becomes imbalanced. Love brings us back to life. Love is, indeed, Life," said Maya, leading me back to the porch.

As we sat down, she revealed the key to a principle that I still use whenever I am in a dilemma. "Knowledge is Light, Love is Life – these are not merely words. By understanding them, you can answer your life's questions. You have gained the knowledge that you hurt your family. That knowledge is your guiding light to what you should do next. Your next step must arise out of love, and life will become better," Maya revealed, all the while looking at me intently.

I nodded because I knew there was only one right way arising out of love. "I must ask for their forgiveness, right?" I asked. "What is your intention in asking for forgiveness?" Maya asked frankly. "I want to feel lighter, get rid of my baggage from the past. I want to feel good about myself again. I am tired of being the culprit in this situation." I confessed. "Then you might not be forgiven, I am afraid," Maya's clear voice announced. I looked at her in confusion. "I don't understand," I said.

What Maya explained to me shifted my mindset forever about relationships and forgiveness. The guru spoke and the disciple listened, "You have an ulterior motive in apologising," she said. "It is all about you, and so, it is selfish. Your intention does not arise from love. Those who need to forgive you will understand that. They might choose not to forgive you and continue to be resentful." I looked at her, and the loss for words showed on my face. Maya's face softened, and I will remain eternally grateful for what she taught me next. "When we apologise, it needs to be less about us and more about the other person. It does not matter what words we choose or how well we speak, the person we care about will focus much deeper than that. They will read our hearts and listen to our feelings. They will look for love. Our intent is more important than content. If our intention is to genuinely improve our life and relationship with that person, then forgiveness will follow sooner or later. We apologise, so we can create a new level of understanding with the other person. Visualise the potential of what can be, not what it is right now or what it was in the past. When the other person feels convinced of our good intentions, they will surely forgive us," Maya said with compassion.

This made a hell of a lot of sense to me now. Hadn't Nina and I used the same principle when we genuinely forgave each other? I was beginning to realise what I needed to do. Solutions might be staring us in the face, and yet, it takes a helping hand to discover them. My excitement was interrupted by Maya's robust voice.

"Why did you and Nina decide to give yourselves another chance?" Maya asked. I was surprised at this sudden change in topic, though I answered her anyway. "After I fell very ill, and had time to think, I saw how I had wasted years of my life chasing the wrong things. My happiness was with Nina first, everything else came second."

"So, you got time to think, and a great decision came your way," said Maya. "That is exactly the point. We need to focus on one thing at a time. Unlike what you might think, this is not a time-consuming process. Rather, it saves a huge amount of time in the long run. That is when knowledge turns into a guiding light. We are at our best when we focus on one goal at a time. Believe me, son, only a minute portion of all our worries put together ever comes true. Be easy on yourself and enjoy this process of transformation," Maya said with a genuine, loving smile. I nodded in agreement and smiled back at her. What she said was absolutely true. Every time I had focussed, I had felt confident of sorting my issues. And when I had allowed too many worries to ride me, I had lost my confidence and felt rudderless. No matter how I rearranged the puzzle, the picture had turned out the same.

Maya now asked me another strange question. "How long do you think you have to live?" Now, who thought about stuff like that? I fumbled for an answer. "Well, I hope to live as long and healthy as you seem to have, Maya."

She nodded and confirmed that she was indeed eighty years old. "If eighty years is your goal, then you have a good thirty more years to live, I guess?" I nodded, wondering what her point was. And, suddenly, I realised what she meant. "Wow, I still have several precious years with my family. My mind was so caught up in the decades already gone by that I forgot about the years I still have with them. Isn't that what you meant?" As I said this, my heart felt lighter. I was smiling again as I happily looked at my teacher.

Maya then made a statement that shook my entire belief system in one stroke. "Imagine your past has chains around you, but you have the key to unlock those chains. When we hold on to the chains of our past, our spirit cannot do its divine work. Let the past go, release it, and let it release you. You will live much longer, believe me. When you choose your future over your past, you have freed yourself. Never worry about the future. Worrying lessens our power greatly. Ask yourself instead: are you ready for a positive beginning to your life? When you say 'yes' to that question, and believe in it truly and deeply, your guilt will turn into the most powerful positive force you can imagine. That force will propel you towards your greatest priority. Don't waste a minute more on beating yourself up. The choice is yours alone. Focus on deciding what is more important to you – self-pity, or self-discovery and awareness? Remember, you have a great life ahead of you that is yet to be lived."

I felt my eyes moisten. I was feeling free and light as a feather. I could fly. My heart was thumping in my chest with excitement and anticipation. All was not lost after all. There was hope. I closed my eyes. "Maya, can I let myself off the hook for my mistakes? Can I possibly forgive myself, you think?" I asked with genuine passion.

Maya's answer still rings in my ears. "Always remember this key to a long, fulfilling, and healthy life. This moment, right here, is to be lived abundantly, with joy, and with gratitude. Always remember that simple principle, Knowledge is Light, Love is Life. Knowledge might stem from our past but guides us to the light of the future, and love reminds us that life is to be lived with joy. You've heard everything. Now I will leave it to you to decide whether you can forgive yourself or not."

As this point, I must share with you something, most of us do not notice in the busy-ness of life. Conditioning is stronger than reality. The environment and messages we grow up with shape our future. That script from childhood dictates our life more than we can imagine. Until one day, a cataclysmic life experience forces us to question our assumptions. Today was that kind of day in my life. The more I saw life as a limiting, tiring, and uphill task, the more I suffered. That was my conditioning holding me back from being my best. I had learned to slog for everything in life. I believed there was no joyful way of achieving success, no easy way to earn money. I believed true peace only belonged to yogis. I was wrong. For the first time in my entire life, I had challenged my assumptions. The answers that were unravelling thrilled me to the core. I felt a kind of confidence that I hadn't known even at the peak of my success.

I was stunned by what Maya had awakened in me. My mind was a whirlwind of thoughts. My emotions were close to the surface now. I felt as if someone had touched my soul in that one moment. For the first time in many years I was listening to myself. There was hope for me, and for all those whose past had been less than perfect. There was light for those who had been blinded by cutthroat competition, and were now tired of keeping up a false image of what they were not. I felt like shouting from the rooftops. Such was my elation, so strong was my hope. There indeed was light at the end of every tunnel.

CHAPTER 3

The Guru Speaks

Quotable Quote: Knowledge is light, love is life

5 Powerful Thoughts

➤ When the vision of our life is beautiful, realising our goals becomes easier

➤ To get new results in our life, we must think new thoughts

➤ Getting entangled in nitty-gritties hides the big picture of our vision. Keep your eyes on the end result.

➤ Love is the most important asset we have, to connect with others, and lead a fulfilling life

➤ A sincere apology creates a new level of understanding with the person we have wronged

The Master Key: Releasing our intention with all our heart enables the Universe to respond in positive ways

Action Point

Forgive yourself and others to clarify your thinking. Let your thinking and planning reflect the right intention, and success will be yours. Put the past behind you and step into your present. Today holds the key to your tomorrow.

Lessons of Chapter Four

Excessive thinking without action is like driving without a destination

Neglect prevents a loving relationship from doing its job – providing love and joy

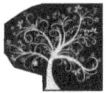

Listening is one of the most powerful ways to resolve issues

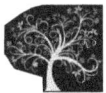

If our heart is in the right place our, words will find the right path and convey the right meaning

Everyone has a spark of brilliance and an understanding of life waiting to be tapped into

CHAPTER 4

An Unlikely Teacher

"Create a definite plan for carrying out your desire, and begin at once, whether you're ready or not, to put it into action."

~Napoleon Hill

As I walked home from Maya's, I felt I was walking on air. I recalled the day I had felt there was no hope in my heart. Today was dramatically different. Life always comes full circle. It was now crystal clear to me what I needed to do first. My understanding of myself and my priorities had to begin at a deep and intimate level. It had to begin with me. Letting myself off the hook and forgiving myself had changed my entire perspective. This was the place I was meant to be at. Our mistakes are part of the path that leads us to our answers. Without them, we would be lost. My mistakes had made me wiser and stronger. I felt ready to overhaul my current life, and make the rest of my life a beautiful experience. I couldn't wait to get started.

I had heard somewhere that excessive thinking without action is like driving without a destination – you are bound to get lost. I had thought enough, and was now ready for action. "How about we go on a vacation? Just the two of us, I mean," I asked Nina casually as we had breakfast together. Her expression saddened and amused me in equal measures. The shock on her face clearly meant neither of us could remember the last time we had taken a vacation as a couple. Nina just stared at me without saying a word. "Fine, I guess you are not interested," I said sipping my tea. "Of course, I am," she replied hastily. I caught her eye, and both of us burst out laughing. I mentally promised myself that this was my time with Nina, and for us to get to know each other all over again. I was going to do everything I could to make it a beautiful memory for both of us.

That weekend, we arrived at a resort in stunning Mauritius, with the silvery beach a short distance away. We got into our holiday gear and set out on a long walk along the beautiful coastline. We returned energised and packed in much more in our day than we had imagined. When we are healthy and fit, we accomplish more in one day than we would normally in three. After a sumptuous meal, Nina decided to try a nearby spa, while I sauntered off to a cafe with a book tucked under my arm. A good book and a cup of hot chai seemed like pure bliss. Books used to be my passion once upon a time. I continued to buy books, but only to stash them fashionably in my office bookshelf. Well, all that was going to change now, I happily thought to myself. Thanks to Maya, I had been reminded of the immeasurable value of reading books. I knew that learning was the key to a fantastic life. What I had learnt a short while ago was already turning my life around in a big way. With that sweet realisation warming my heart, I entered a quiet cafe and chose a table that faced the sea, with waves breaking along the pristine beach. Sipping a rejuvenating cup of tea, I opened the first page of my book. I was in heaven! We don't really need a million dollars to have fun, I thought with a chuckle.

I was still engrossed in my book, when I heard someone sit down at the table next to me. It was a young man, about twenty or so. I nodded at him, and he smiled back politely. Just as I was about to get lost in my book again, his phone rang. I couldn't help overhearing as he sharply spoke into his phone. "Dad, I really wish you wouldn't keep calling me. I said I don't want to talk about this, okay? That's it, all right? I don't care what you think, this is my life. I thought we were done with this topic." With that he clicked his phone shut and threw his arms in the air in exasperation. I couldn't help sympathise with his invisible father whose call had just been hung up by his son. I still don't know what came over me, but I asked him an obvious question. "You seem really upset with your father?" He looked at me surprised, and quickly brushed aside my comment. "Nothing serious, my dad is just bugging me about something I don't want to do."

"It's amazing how all parents specialise in meddling with their children's lives, huh," I said chuckling. Mike gave me a tight smile, and I saw pain written across his young face. There was an awkward silence, in which, I got plenty of time to regret my tactless remark. While I was thinking of how to get out of this conversation, I heard him speak again. "Are you a parent by any chance?"

"Yes, I am. I have two beautiful children," I said. "Well, then maybe, you can answer something for me. By the way, I am Mike," he said curtly. I nodded, and introduced myself.

"So, where were we? Yeah, parents are experts in the interference department. First, they bring you into this world, and then, expect you to pay them back for the rest of your life. What's the use of having parents that are selfish? They always see things from their point of view, and it doesn't matter to them, what makes me happy. They are so worried about their darned image. I think, I am just an embarrassment to them. They are trying to 'deal' with me – over the phone! What do you have to say about parents like that, now?"

As I heard this young man, my mind raced back to some of the mistakes I had made with my own children. I suspected, I wasn't any better than Mike's parents. Wasn't I also trying to deal with my kids over the phone? Continued neglect prevents a loving relationship from providing love and joy. I was guilty of it myself. I frowned, as I focused on what he had asked me. "Mike, I am curious to know what it is that you want to do. Is it really that bad?" Mike thought for a while and hesitatingly shared. "As far as I am concerned, that's the best thing I can do with my life. I want to become a successful painter. I have been painting for years, and I know I can make it big some day."

"So, your folks are unhappy with your career choice, is that the issue?" I asked trying to put myself in their shoes. "Yeah, sums it up pretty much. They want me to have a more respectable career than fiddling around with a brush, I guess. Both my parents spent their life chasing success, and never had the time to ask me what I really wanted to do, what would make me happy? Just because their friends' children are going the corporate way, doesn't mean I have to be sacrificed to keep up their social image," Mike said with a grimace.

His words went through my heart like a sharp knife. Mike had just nailed the mistake most parents make when they unwittingly begin to use their children's achievements to get social mileage. I knew in my heart, that we set our children up for success, when we nurture their innate abilities and talents. Had I not followed that myself?

"Are you happy with your children and what they are doing?" Mike's sudden question brought me back to the present. This was a completely unexpected situation, and I squirmed in my chair. "I am proud of my two children, but I wish they would do a few things differently. My daughter hardly ever speaks to me, and my son's school complained about his partying. I just want the best for them," I said with a sigh. Mike looked at me suspiciously. "I seriously doubt if my parents truly want the best for me when they go around pushing their own agenda," he said, looking decidedly unhappy at his bitter analysis.

My heart suddenly softened towards Mike, I doubt if anyone had genuinely heard him out so far. Listening is one of the most powerful ways to resolve issues. So, here I was on my vacation, and as irony would have it, busy trying to counsel someone else's kid. Blame my paternal instincts, but I couldn't help asking him an important question. "Mike, do you think your parents deserve another chance? I am not sure if you ever explained to them what you just did to me. Do you seriously believe your parents are out to give you grief?" Mike looked far into the sea and thought about this for several moments. Finally, turning to me he said something that warmed my heart. "I love my parents. Heck, they are my parents. I do want to give them a chance, and I want them to hear me out. But, what if they reject me? I know they are disappointed with me. They will never forgive me for going against their wishes."

At this point Maya's startling truths about forgiveness were swirling in my mind. She was so right, that there was hardly a new age problem that did not have an answer in age-old wisdom. On an impulse, I decided to share some of that wisdom with Mike today. "I see some of my own son in you, so I hope you will take it in the right spirit. Having the right intention and true forgiveness are such powerful forces, that our tiny thoughts about rejection and acceptance are insignificant in comparison." Mike looked at me questioningly. "You need to do your job, which as I see it, is to visit your parents, and honestly share with them the plans you have for your life. Explain to them calmly your intention to be a great painter. Mike, the key question is; do you have it in your heart to genuinely forgive your parents? Whether your parents accept or reject your choices is not for you to worry about. In intimately emotional issues our intent matters more than our petty concerns for desirable consequences. If our heart is in the right place, our words will find the right path and convey the right meaning. Your job is just this, nothing more and nothing less. I wish my son and daughter would forgive me. I might have made the same mistakes with them that you just spoke about. I'd love to get another chance at being a better dad to my kids." I cautiously looked at him, and wondered if I had revealed more than I should have. Mike nodded and gave me a smile. He was watching me thoughtfully, and I was sure I had put my foot in my mouth.

He leaned toward me, and I felt his young hand on my shoulder. "I think you should talk to your son and daughter, just come clean with them," he said with far more maturity than I had expected of him. "Huh? How do you mean?" I asked genuinely puzzled. "Don't make excuses for what happened in the past, kids hate that kind of covering up, believe me. They will respect you if you tell them the truth, and that you regret it now. I can vouch for that. Come to think of it, the wisdom you shared with me must work for all of us, right? So, just like my parents, you also deserve another chance, and so do your kids. I don't know them, but even if they are doing something wrong, is there a point in making them feel rotten about it? Maybe your kids will like you better if you take some honest interest in the good stuff they do, you know. And don't care about what others will say. Kids aren't trophies. They are there so all of you can be family."

I sat there in shock and awe as I realised, how Mike's uncomplicated thinking had simplified my painful problem. He was one of the most unlikely teachers I could have hoped to come across. Everyone has a spark of brilliance and an understanding of life waiting to be tapped. I might have given him a perspective about his parents, but he had given me a huge gift. I looked at Mike's young face with renewed respect. Wisdom is not related to age, it's only related to what we make of our experiences. Mike had hit upon a truth that had elevated his status to a 'teacher' in my life.

I hurried back to our room and told Nina everything that had transpired over my tea trip to the cafe. The haze had lifted from my mind, and I couldn't wait to visit our children and talk to them. That night, Nina and I sat on the beach watching the calm dark sea, and it struck me how our life was expansive, it was abundant. Our responsibility was to enjoy our blessings and not disregard them with our negative and critical ways. I just needed to reach out and accept the help available all around me. Maya and Mike had crossed my path for a reason, I was certain of that. I had asked for help with deep sincerity, and my prayers were being answered abundantly.

CHAPTER 4

An Unlikely Teacher

Quotable Quote: Excessive thinking without action is like driving without a destination

5 Powerful Thoughts

➤ We don't need a million dollars to have a great time every single day

➤ Continued neglect prevents relationships from giving love and joy

➤ Listening is a great way to resolve issues rather than blaming each other

➤ If our heart is in the right place, words find their way when we speak

➤ Everyone has a spark of brilliance. Both, the young and the old, have wisdom

The Master Key: Treating our mistakes in life as a necessary step leads us to the right path

Action Point

Take action based on your desires with complete conviction. Feel confident that help is available and good people are in abundance. Focus on the positives in any situation and expect the best to happen.

LESSONS OF CHAPTER FIVE

A deep sense of gratitude enables us to visualise our future with clarity and purpose

External situations can affect a relationship, but positive emotions and inner will always decide the results

When we feel absolute internal joy and confidence, the entire Universe turns its attention on us

To get desirable and positive results we must first sow them in our hearts, and the mind will be convinced of their reality

CHAPTER 5

Path to a Fulfilling Life

"When you affirm big, believe big and pray big, putting faith into action, big things happen."

~Norman Vincent Peale

Nina and my recent trip triggered some dramatic changes in our lives. With the help of my teachers I was beginning to think more positively and clearly than I had in my entire life. Since then, I've learnt a useful lesson – we don't have to reach perfection to feel great about our lives. It is like chasing glittering sand in a desert in the hope of finding water, only to be disappointed again and again. Our eternal spirit has the power to make our lives complete and happy at any time. It does not need a perfect time to provide joy. I have come to believe that our life is to be enjoyed and lived right now, in this moment. A deep sense of gratitude about our lives helps us visualise our future with clarity and purpose. Astounding success and unimaginable happiness then comes to us in abundance. In fact, our lives are meant to become magnificently successful and gratifying.

I began to live according to this understanding. As they say, one great execution is worth a thousand plans. If I could put in action the plan that was brewing in my mind, I knew some great results might follow. A fantastic life was unfolding right before my eyes, and I was the master craftsman. Nina and I shared an unspoken understanding that our relationship had reached a new high. I think nothing in life brings two loved ones closer than a crisis, and nothing can tear them apart faster than a crisis too. The difference lies in our attitude. We had faced our final crisis with faith, holding each other's hands, as our hearts firmly believed in the results we desired together. External situations can affect a relationship, but positive emotions and inner will always decide the results. Our new life together had given me the strength to take the next step forward.

I knew that a conversation with my good friend, Maya, would help me decide my next course of action. I visited her the same evening. In her usual perceptive way, she had understood that I had something on my mind. "It might sound dramatic, Maya, but it seems the Universe has heard my prayers, and is sending help from all directions to make my life happier every day." I then shared with her my chance meeting with Mike, and what he had said to me in Mauritius. Maya agreed. "You seem to have met a very wise young person indeed. Honesty with loved ones is the best way to forge stronger relationships. Many of us wrongly believe that lying and hiding information keeps everyone happy. Nothing could be further from the truth." I agreed with her. Mike's point about communicating with my children had changed my entire approach to building bridges with them.

Though I felt happy, I knew there were some major areas of my life I was yet to tackle. "There is still the issue of my life at work," I said to Maya hesitatingly. "At times, I wonder if I should just quit, but then, wouldn't that be unfair? My team has been working crazy schedules because they have seen me do the same. There has to be a middle path." I looked at Maya and shrugged.

My trusted teacher went about resolving my question in her typical way, with which I was now very familiar. "How did you sort out your life at home so far?" I mulled this over. "Funny you ask me that. Frankly, life has flowed seamlessly since we first met. I now truly believe that the positivity inside me is working for my benefit. It keeps giving me one clue after the other, and success has followed. My intuition about my next step has not failed me so far. I felt pure bliss and absolute joy when my wife and I forgave each other. The purpose of our lives became crystal clear. It's been pretty smooth from that point on. Both of us are having immense fun with the process of transformation."

"Bravo! You have already discovered what you need to do at work. So, why ask for my help?" Maya said cheerfully. I looked at her in exasperation, and was about to ask her to spell it out for me, when a brilliant realisation hit me like a ton of bricks. I had discovered the secret, after all. "The transformation I am looking for is in my hands. What I have done at a personal level is what I need to do with my life outside. The principle of change remains the same, doesn't it?"

I spoke quickly, brimming with excitement. Maya smiled, and nodded silently. She was excited and thoughtful all at the same time. "You should be very proud of yourself for discovering this gem of wisdom through your own personal journey. I find it unfortunate that what is so easy and fundamental, is complicated by our lack of understanding of basic principles," she remarked.

"How do you mean?" I asked, wanting to dig deeper. "I wish more people knew what you have just discovered. The four magic actions we need to take to transform any area of our life are no mystery. They are meant to be part of this divine life we have, and bring us immense joy and success. Our life has a spiritual purpose, with or without our consent, and this is why we have at our disposal these four magical steps:

First, we must let go of past hurts and mistakes as they cloud our judgement and corrupt our intent in seeking change.

63

Second, we need to be clear about our objectives. We must reach a point of absolute clarity without a shadow of doubt or confusion.

Third, our mind should be able to visualise our success so powerfully that we know in our hearts, there is no option, but to succeed. Nothing can shake our confidence then.

The fourth and final step is to follow our heart and take inspired action. We must put our plans in action and enjoy the process. In fact, the last step reveals itself to us.

"Wouldn't you agree that it's a simple and fun process?" Maya asked.

"What do you mean by inspired action revealing itself? Don't we have to work hard to get into action? The last step should be the toughest," I said doubtfully.

Maya shook her head. "The last step is the easiest because it is the natural end result of the first three steps. The eternal spirit within each of us is an extension of the Universe. When we feel absolute joy and confidence, the entire Universe turns its attention upon us. This force creates such opportunities that anything we set as our purpose will come true. The nature of our Universe is positive. It is the greatest living, pulsating source of creative energy available to us. We unite with its power naturally and easily when we forgive others, have a strong purpose, and move towards that purpose with absolute confidence."

I felt as if some long forgotten truths of my life were awakening from a deep slumber. It was unbelievable that I had travelled through several countries, met countless intelligent men and women, only to discover these mega truths through my aged neighbour. Our greatest power was right here, in the depths of our joyful spirit. It was patiently waiting for us to call it into action and to help us reach our highest goals.

I couldn't resist asking Maya what I had seen happening to several of my own friends. "In my experience, many confident and smart people fail at their goals. I am sure they work hard too. Why does that happen?"

Maya's answer was not just simple, but obvious, now that I think about it. It opened my mind to unlimited possibilities in my own future. "We fail when we forget to unite with the power of the Universe. Even if we bring several intelligent people together, they won't succeed without first creating a bridge with the Universe. This is precisely why most people who argue and blame each other, never reach their most creative potential. Our Universe does not respond positively to anything that arises from negative intent, however hard we try or confident we might be. Let us say, you do not believe in your purpose and lack the vision of an improved personal life, but you work very hard at it anyway. Will that work?" I shook my head thoughtfully.

"Precisely," Maya emphasised. "To get desirable and positive results, we first have to sow them in our hearts, and our mind will be convinced of their reality. The rest will be joyful work, not slogging. Every shred of help will then reach us at lightning speed, and nothing short of miracles will happen. In fact, it is funny how we call these miracles mere coincidences. There is nothing like a chance happening. We bring all our happiness and all our pain upon ourselves."

This was nature's law according to Maya's age-old wisdom. Considering, I had faltered with sowing the right seeds myself, I was convinced of what Maya had just said to me.

I felt like an excited child who had just discovered a bunch of new toys tucked away in a forgotten cupboard. I had received invaluable wisdom, and my mind was buzzing with new ideas and hope for the future. Like that wise Eastern saying, my guru had not just given me a fish to eat, she had taught me how to fish. I was now on my way to discovering my own truths.

"Maya, I don't think I can ever repay you for the knowledge you have selflessly bestowed on me. Is there anything I can do in return? You just have to name it." Maya became silent for a while, then asked me to do something rather curious. "I will be very happy if you can visit a man whose address I will give you. He lives not far from the city, in the countryside. I cannot reveal his name to you right now, but if you trust me, then please go and meet him."

I stood in her doorway trying to understand this mysterious request to meet a stranger whose identity was to remain unknown until I met him. Still, I told Maya that I would do as she wished, and would visit this man next weekend. As I walked back home, I understood that change was a journey to be enjoyed. I had played safe all my life and stayed in a comfort zone defined by my limiting beliefs. Now, I could tap the potential of my life.

My future was just beginning.

CHAPTER 5

Path to a Fulfilling Life

Quotable Quote: Our mind must visualise success, so we have no option, but to succeed

5 Powerful Thoughts

➤ Your greatest power lies in the depths of your joyful spirit. It gives rise to positive thoughts and actions.

➤ You don't have to reach perfection to feel great. Joy needs to be an everyday habit.

➤ You are meant to become magnificently successful. Success is a natural consequence of faith.

➤ To get desirable results we have to sow them in our heart first

➤ Negative intent never produces positive outcomes

The Master Key: Abundant inner joy and confidence, attracts the attention of the entire Universe to help us succeed

Action Point

Unite with the power of the Universe by nurturing positive thoughts and feelings. Feel the joy you deserve. Hold on to your purpose, and move forward with faith. Inspired action leads to spectacular success.

LESSONS OF CHAPTER SIX

Keeping up our curiosity results in a healthier life

It's okay to be poor of money, but it's unforgivable to be poor of ideas

Being busy is not equal to being satisfied

Misfortunes are absolutely necessary, without them we would be lesser people

Life is what we have in the moment; life is present in all its glory right now

CHAPTER 6

Meeting a Secret Stranger

"A dream is your creative vision for your life in the future. You must break out of your current comfort zone and become comfortable with the unfamiliar and the unknown."

~Denis Waitley

That Friday, I remembered my promise to Maya about visiting her friend. As I neared her home, I caught a burst of fragrance from her beautiful and colourful garden. She sure knew how to nurture life, I thought, smiling. She came bustling out of her home with an apron on. Apparently, Maya was baking cookies to take to an orphanage nearby. I marvelled at the relentless energy and passion that kept her going at her age. I was too embarrassed to even admit that I knew nothing about this orphanage that was right in our neighbourhood. I sure had loads to learn from her.

Maya happily handed me a piece of paper with an address. I noticed that she had pointedly omitted the name of the person I was to visit. I gave her a reproachful look, but she refused to divulge the name. As usual, she was not going to make this easy for me. The address was of a farmhouse about one hour away from the city. Wishing her a great weekend, I carefully slipped the piece of paper in my wallet and walked back home. I wondered what mystery awaited me the next day.

As Nina and I started out to meet the mystery man, I felt the rush of a brand new experience. This was a bizarre situation. I almost felt like a child again, when I used to love going on treasure hunts with my friends. I could still remember the thrill of finding a clue behind a bush that led us to the next one, and the joy of getting to our treasure. This experience was proving to be every bit as exciting, and I found myself looking forward to solving this mystery. I now understand how a child-like curiosity results in a healthy life. Nina was happy to come along for the sheer opportunity to go on a long drive, even if it meant meeting a stranger for an unknown purpose.

The beautiful drive reminded us of our early days together when long drives were a must every week. I wonder why our expressions of love and caring reduce with advancing years. I felt humbled by my recent discoveries about love and life. Thanks to my teachers and my wonderful wife, I now knew that as we grow older, so must our gestures of love and devotion. We need them much more when we are older than when we are young. Every moment spent with my family was a blessing. I looked at Nina with absolute love in my heart as she gave me a huge smile.

Time flew, and before I knew it, we had already reached the farmhouse that Maya had directed me to. A board simply said, 'Marigold Farms'. Well, that didn't help because the name obviously came from the innumerable, brilliant yellow marigold flowers that lined the driveway. We still didn't know who owned this farm. As we drove along the winding driveway I looked out and realised we had entered an extraordinary place. Rows upon rows of lush grape vines, weighed down by mouth-watering grapes peppered the landscape. They seemed to go on for as far as the eye could see. We had entered a stunning vineyard! Nina looked at me with disbelief as we leaned out of the window to drink in the heady fragrance of fruits and flowers.

The driveway ended at a charming farmhouse with a large covered porch framed by flowering creepers. My curiosity was killing me now. Who could this person be? Just then, a door swung open, and we saw a smart, average-built man with salt and pepper hair, briskly walk out. He had a big smile on his pleasant face as he approached us. My jaw dropped in surprise. Of course I knew this person, he was no mystery! I was staring at a man who was a legend in the wine-making business. His face was as well known as the prime minister of this country. There was no mistaking Kian - the King-of-Wine!

"Hi there, I am Kian. It's great to have you both here," he said extending his hand. I gathered myself as we introduced ourselves. Kian's wife, Lina, also came out to greet us. I wondered how Maya knew such a noted businessman, and had felt comfortable sending us to his home. "So, how do you know Maya? I must say, she's a gem of a person," I asked curiously as we all sat down in the beautiful porch. Kian burst out laughing. "That's so typical of my mother. I bet she must be chuckling at her little prank." I sat dumbstruck as it sank in that Kian was Maya's son! We gaped at him. This was too improbable. Of all the people who could have been my neighbour, Maya had to be it. Maya was Kian's mother! I shook my head in disbelief for a second time within five minutes as everyone laughed some more.

Kian and I were left together to chat as Lina took Nina on a tour of the beautiful vineyard. There were so many interesting questions I wanted to ask him. The media was full of the mystique around his life and his meteoric rise. Many years ago, Kian was the head of a well-known telecom giant before he quit and vanished for the next five years. He came back with a bang, and now owned one of the most well-respected wine brands in the country.

I roughly knew him to be about sixty years old. Though, I doubted that as I sat facing him. Kian seemed much younger and more spirited than most people are at sixty. He wasn't even as grey haired or wrinkled. He seemed super-fit with no trace of extra flab. What jumped out was his genuine aura of happiness and peace. Kian radiated a calm and contented vibe, and I got this weird feeling that I was speaking to a yogi. He was an improbable choice for a multimillionaire businessman. There was nothing of the flamboyance, frantic pace, or overflowing energy that people associate with business tycoons.

"I hope you don't mind my asking, Kian, but is this why you quit your job – to start a wine-making business?" I asked, half-afraid he might refuse to answer me. He smiled at my observation and put me at ease instantly. "Honestly, I wish I had this whole brainwave much earlier. It's okay to be poor of money, but it's unforgivable to be poor of ideas, isn't it? If I had paid heed to some early signs, I could have saved myself a lot of heartburn. I hope you are luckier than me, I had kind of lost my way." As he made this candid observation, my mind raced back to my own breakdown not far in the past. I too had lost my way. Thankfully, I had survived my warning bell, and the Universe had given me a chance to reinvent my life. That happy chain of events had led me to this place. And I knew I was going to walk out with some fantastic new thoughts to work on.

"I would love to hear more about your transformational journey, Kian. I am sure there is something in it for me to learn," I said humbly. He seemed almost thankful to share his story with someone. After many chats with Maya, I knew what a relief it was to share our pain with another.

"I don't mind saying that I was living the life of a fool. I thought I had the world at my feet, and nothing could spoil my dream life. I was wrong, very wrong. Money and greed had blinded me. You know, I lost my father while I was on one of my innumerable business trips abroad. That really broke my spirit. He was seventy-five years old, and fell ill the day I was to leave, but I chose work and travelled anyway. I had this irrational belief that parents are always there for us, and my father would be fine even before I came back. Not to mention, I couldn't imagine cancelling an appointment with the head of the world's largest telecom firm. In my unending ambition, I believed that my work priorities justified all my actions. I lost my father the next day, and I couldn't even say goodbye," Kian sighed as he recollected his painful past.

I could almost feel his ache. I found it hard to believe that I was sitting in front of a man who was once a formidable and shrewd leader. He seemed as vulnerable and ordinary as a vegetable-seller on the street who had learnt the rules of life the hard way. "I am sorry to hear that, Kian. I can well imagine your painful though evolutionary journey up until now. You have been very brave. What you have achieved is tremendous. This farm is stunning, and your brand is known to even a kid in this country," I said.

Kian nodded in acknowledgement of my sincere compliment. "Work that saps your physical, spiritual, and mental energy is never worth it. Thankfully, this farm gave me a way out. I love this place; I love the work we do here. Wine-making is as much an art as a skill. I work in nature, and this vineyard you see is not just a business for me. It is part of my personal goal to achieve spiritual and mental growth. I still do the meanest of tasks on my vineyard and get my hands dirty. Believe me, it is not just liberating, it keeps me grounded as well. It reminds me that I am just an ordinary man producing extraordinary wine." Kian revealed. Suddenly he blushed and looked at me with a child's open gaze. "I sincerely hope I am not boring you with my wine philosophy," he chuckled. I shook my head. "Believe me, whatever you have said resonates completely with what I have recently learned. I am excited and honoured to be hearing it from you directly. I have much to learn still. Please go on," I said with genuine gratitude.

Kian continued. "I had sunk deep into the success trap. We must watch out for the disease of instant gratification, brother. It can consume our imagination and vision. Strength lies in better, not in bigger or more. Quality is far more important than quantity. Clichéd, but true to the core. It took me a while to realise that, but this philosophy drives my entire business now," he shared.

A question suddenly struck me. "Was it tough to begin a new business? Do you miss the action of being in a big job? After all, handling a buzzing company is totally different from running a farm. And growing grapes is not exactly a replacement for the high adrenaline corporate life you had."

Kian nodded vigorously. "I am sure I would have asked you the same question if I were in your place. Frankly, I was so used to being busy that I felt lost without my job. Yet, going back to a hectic lifestyle in a big city was just not my cup of tea. I didn't hear my inner voice saying 'yes'. When grief hit me, something tremendous happened to my belief system. It dawned on me that being busy wasn't equal to being satisfied. We could be very busy in a high-flying job, and yet be empty, unhappy people. It might sound a bit funny to you, but it almost felt as if thoughts that had remained dormant within me until then, had awakened to some kind of personal enlightenment.

"I now know that excessive physical gratification ruins spiritual satisfaction. There is a strong connection there, and I am not a saint, but I know this to be true through my own experience. It is phenomenal how grief can awaken our deepest emotions, and therefore, our spiritual life. I felt so sorted out at the end of my ordeal. I went through a lot of personal pain, but it made me completely clear about my priorities. Misfortunes are absolutely necessary, for without them, we would be lesser people."

What he said surprised me greatly. "Most people I know try to avoid pain and misfortune at any cost," I commented. "That's true," he said, "and I wouldn't wish pain and guilt on anyone. I don't mean we go looking for the bad stuff, but hey, who doesn't have their fair share of tragedies and failures in life? We all go through our dark days. The key is to grab the opportunity to change our beliefs about life and success when we fail. There is no shame in falling down – only in failing to get up again, dusting ourselves, and moving on. If we don't, life will pass us by anyway. Only, this time, we'll end up more of a failure."

I sat there watching Kian with renewed respect as he made these profound statements. Wasn't this my story as well? My misfortunes had taught me some of the best lessons I could have learnt. Life indeed was strange, and maybe, we all needed a jolt once in a while to wake us up. I had certainly deserved, and got, one.

As I mulled over what Kian had shared, I felt confident that his transformation wasn't a fluke. There had to be something more to his story. I wondered what had helped him achieve both mental peace and material success. "From everything I have heard from you Kian, you seem to have done a perfect balancing act in terms of redefining your life and career. What is your mantra? You see, I am at similar crossroads in my life. I will really appreciate any tips from you," I confessed. I knew his answer was going to take me a long way, and I leaned forward hopefully.

"I got back to basics," he announced mysteriously. I saw Kian's face glow as if a great memory had welled up within him and filled him with happiness and peace. "You seem to have attained nirvana! I can't wait to hear what happened to you. It must have been something special," I quipped. He looked excited and his eyes twinkled. Watching him reminded me of Maya instantly!

"I realised something extremely important. Life is what we have in the moment; life is present in all its glory, right now," Kian began to explain. "I stopped relying on the uncertainty of an elusive tomorrow. For years now, Lina and I make it our priority to wake up every morning and promise ourselves to live our life fully that day. You know, living life everyday is much tougher than just leaning back and watching TV. It takes effort and commitment. You cannot imagine what this 'live-your-life-fully-today' philosophy has done for us, it is phenomenal. The idea to begin this vineyard came to us effortlessly, while we were on one of our long drives outside town. Before we knew it, we had acquired this land and started cultivation. The same strategy has helped us to not magnify our problems, but to actively seek resolutions.

"We've been able to keep our perspective even in tough times. I can say with absolute confidence that we have had hundreds more happy moments than we have had sad ones in the last few years. Every morning we get an opportunity either to exist, or to truly live our lives. Our intention is to live completely, every single day. At the end of the day, we never forget to be thankful for all the blessings we have. Gratitude is the key to a happy and fulfilling life. Might sound simplistic to you, but it works like magic. In fact, why don't you try this brilliant method? Just spend the next week saying more thank yous than you've ever said in one week. Show gratitude when no one expects you to. Say a big 'thank you' to the grocery chap who makes fresh vegetables available to you. Wake up really early tomorrow morning and give a big smile to your newspaper guy. I bet he hasn't got that from anyone in a long time! Say 'thank you' to the person who cleans your street everyday. Smile at the liftman who ensures you reach your floor. Just give this a shot for the next seven days and let me know how it feels."

Kian looked totally happy as he shared his success mantra with me. He was bang on target. Nina and I were increasingly enjoying the blessings in our lives rather than fretting over the past. We were certainly happier than before. I understood Kian's 'thank-you-strategy,' too. I had never thanked the people who cleaned up after me, or brought me all kinds of things to my doorstep. Then and there, I resolved to be more grateful to the people around me.

Glancing at Kian's face I knew I had found my answer to why he looked young and so full of life. When you discover your purpose, you grow younger, not older. He had discovered and followed his heart's desire. I now needed to find my own heart's desire. I knew I was closer to my life's purpose now than ever before. Our trip to meet the mysterious host had been a far greater adventure than I had hoped for. Life's jigsaw pieces were finally falling into place. I had found my treasure, after all.

CHAPTER 6

Meeting a Secret Stranger

Quotable Quote: Every morning we get an opportunity either to simply exist, or to truly live our lives

5 Powerful Thoughts

➤ Keeping up our curiosity results in a healthy and happy life

➤ Work that saps our physical, spiritual, and mental energy is not worth it

➤ The disease of instant gratification eats up our vision and imagination. Money is important, but life is more important.

➤ Being busy is not equal to being satisfied. We can be very busy and very unproductive.

➤ Gratitude is the key to living a fulfilling life. Saying 'thank you' opens up our hearts.

The Master Key: Discovering our purpose and pursuing it with passion helps us grow younger, not older

Action Point

Focus on living your life fully today. Carefully examine your work ethic, and keep away from instant gratification. Avoid magnifying your problems, and actively seek to resolve them.

Lessons of Chapter Seven

There is no perfect time to make a new beginning

When we truly connect with others we don't need to convince them

Taking responsibility for our lives is the greatest self-gift

Honesty is a great way of giving our relationships another chance

CHAPTER 7

A Family Reunited

"Our most basic instinct is not for survival but for family. Most of us would give our own life for the survival of a family member, yet we lead our daily life too often as if we take our family for granted."

~Paul Pearshall

I was counting my blessings so much more after returning from our adventure. It is difficult to describe the surge of happiness and contentment I felt when I thanked anyone. I got a lot of surprised looks, but that didn't deter me. I knew I was doing this as much for myself as for them. Our meeting with Kian had opened up enormous doors in my mind. I felt more alive and creative than I can express here. Little did we know that more surprises were in store for us!

One morning as I was getting dressed for work, I felt I had gathered enough self-respect, personal power, and clarity to sound credible to my children. As I share this part of my story with you, I am tempted to give you a peek into an exciting adventure that happened soon after I met my kids. That experience, which I will share with you in the next chapter, is an inseparable part of my life's story. It is critical to let you know of the entirely unexpected wisdom that came my way in the most improbable of places. But I must get through the important first part of my story before I take you to that spectacular second part.

You might find this debatable, but I don't think there is a perfect time to make a new beginning. Even then, I chose to wait for the right moment to make my trip to meet my kids, Anya and Neil. It had only been a month since my chat with Mike in Mauritius, but his simple words of wisdom still rang in my ears. In the short time that had passed, a huge transformation had taken place in my beliefs and actions. I was no longer the person my children had rejected.

To make sure that my intentions in meeting Anya and Neil were correct, I chose a long weekend to plan our trip. I saw no appeal in billing my company for an investment that was about to reunite me with my children. I wanted to hold my head high when we told them we had come over just to meet them. I hoped and prayed in my heart that we could reunite as a family again. Nina had tears in her eyes when I shared my intention with her. She nodded, and gave me a silent hug. As we stood there holding each other, I thought of all the years I had wasted. But it did not bring on pangs of guilt anymore. Like Maya had said, my guilt had become the biggest positive force of my life. I was living in the present and letting my spirit guide me to the future. Nothing in my past was worth wasting my present over. Our today is indeed a gift bestowed on us.

That weekend, as Nina and I boarded our flight to New York, I wondered what would have been my mindset if I hadn't met the wise Maya, the brave Kian, my young teacher, Mike, and my forgiving wife, Nina. I felt absolutely confident of my intention in meeting my children now. I was not worried about putting up an image tailored to their acceptance. I had no pre-planned dialogues to impress or convince my children. Most importantly, I felt no need to emotionally blackmail them into forgiving me. When you truly connect with others, you don't need to convince them. I was enjoying our long journey, and felt utmost faith that this trip was about to become a loving experience for all of us. I leaned back in my seat, and looking out of the tiny window of the aircraft, thanked the Universe with all my heart.

Neil and Anya were happy, confused, and upset at seeing us, all at the same time, if that's possible. Neil was nothing like what we had expected. He had turned into a responsible, sober, and engaging young man. At least we didn't see him rolling around in a drunken stupor. That is not to say that the reports we had got from his school had been false. Something had changed Neil quite significantly. We found out that not too far in the past, Neil had landed up in his classroom still slightly drunk. His professor found this out, but decided to give our son a last chance.

"I wonder how the son of such a diligent and illustrious father such as yours could turn out like this," said the professor. "Let alone making your parents proud of you, I hope you can be proud of yourself someday. Life is giving you another chance, Neil. Think about it." That caustic but truthful remark had hit our son more than any reprimands from us could have. Neil had succeeded in cleaning up his act. At times, just one thought can revolutionise our habits, and therefore, our destiny. Taking responsibility for our lives is the greatest self-gift, and Neil had gifted himself his future.

As far as our daughter Anya was concerned, I was both happy and sad to note that she wasn't my little girl anymore. Anya was a beautiful young woman. She had taken entirely after Nina, something I was very proud of. She sat silently with her face turned away, and I saw two tiny tears appear in the corners of her lovely eyes. Initially, Anya was suspicious of our visit. As we persevered, she gradually began to open up about her life. I understood the wisdom of Maya's advice – it is best to do our job and leave forgiveness to the person we have wronged.

A couple of days into our trip, I found a quiet opportunity when all four of us were together, and decided to speak my heart out. "Anya, Neil, I have something to say to both of you." Our children exchanged a worried glance and looked back at me. "One of the main reasons we came here was to meet both of you, of course. The other reason is that I need to apologise for the pain that I know I have caused you over the years." Anya's eyes widened in surprise as she quickly looked at her mother. Nina smiled at her gently, almost as if assuring our daughter that I hadn't lost my marbles, yet. I took a deep breath and continued. "I know I've missed the years when you were growing up. In the bargain, I burdened your mother with responsibilities that I should have shared with her equally.

"I don't blame my job. I blame myself for my obsession and addiction to work. Believe me, I will never wish for either of you to work the way I did, no matter how much money or prestige you can earn. I know our personal goals so much better now. Both of you are one of our greatest priorities. All we want is for the four of us to remain connected. A family is about being there for each other and knowing that there is love in our hearts. In fact, these are perhaps the happiest two days we can remember with both of you. You should go ahead and do what makes you happy in your life and your career. After seeing you, I know we can trust your judgement, and that you will do the right thing. You can't imagine how proud we are of both of you already. And that is all I wanted to say, I really hope you will understand our intention in making this surprise trip to see you."

I had finally come clean with my children. No excuses, no justifications, just the hard truth. Honesty is a great way of giving relationships another chance. What I had said to them would have been impossible if I had a selfish, self-serving agenda on my mind. I wasn't desperately waiting for their forgiveness; this was my test not theirs. I had served the purpose for which we had come here. Mike would have been proud of me, I thought. I hoped that he had found it in his heart to forgive his parents, as well.

For a few moments there was absolute silence as our children pondered over what I had said. My son finally nodded, and gave me a warm hug, thumping me on the back. Anya sat as if rooted to her seat, looking at me with unimaginable love and affection. I saw tears in my children's eyes. I held both of them in a tight hug, and felt my eyes moisten with love for the three most important people in my life. Nina put her arm around me reassuringly. Today was one of the happiest days of our lives. We were reconnected as loved ones are meant to be. We were a family once again.

CHAPTER 7

A Family Reunited

Quotable Quote: When we truly connect with others we don't need to convince them

5 Powerful Thoughts

➤ There is no perfect time to make a new beginning. Today, this moment, is the right one.

➤ Our guilt can become the biggest positive force of our life. It can propel us to do our best to make our future brighter.

➤ Nothing in our past is worth wasting our present over. Look ahead, and step forward.

➤ Just one thought can revolutionise our habits and our destiny. One spark is enough to ignite the fire within.

➤ Taking responsibility for our lives is the greatest self-gift. Stop blaming, and start moving.

The Master Key: Breathing honesty into our relationships, gives them a new life

Action Point

Nurture your most important relationships. Remain honest and loving in your communication. What you are at home will dictate who you become on the outside.

LESSONS OF CHAPTER EIGHT

Life is meaningful only when we explore the possibilities

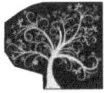

When we believe in ourselves, the world follows us

Making a difference to others while we pursue our goals is a natural expression of our higher purpose

Our supreme purpose is to live a happy and complete life, full of loving relationships

CHAPTER 8

Message in the Mountains

"You can conquer almost any fear if you will make up your mind to do so. For remember, fear doesn't exist anywhere except in the mind."

~Dale Carnegie

As promised, here is the second part of my final story, that is so spectacular, I still wonder if it really happened to me. Reuniting as a family was one of the best decisions we had taken. The joy of doing something with courage and an open heart had become evident to me now. Nina and I had returned from New York, but my bond with our two children was growing stronger with every passing day. A phone call or email from them filled my heart with love and gratitude. Our closeness inspired Anya and Neil to visit us in India for a family vacation. You might agree that vacations are the first casualty of a workaholic lifestyle. Almost on an impulse, we decided to travel north to see the beautiful mountains. The day arrived when our holiday would start. I couldn't wait to get to the little mountain town we were headed to, from where, the grand Himalayan range was fantastically visible.

The ride up the mountain roads was thrilling and rejuvenating. We couldn't stop taking photos and video of the stunning vistas that exploded on the horizon as we went higher and higher. We finally checked into our resort late in the evening. I looked out, but all I could see was darkness, though, the refreshing smells of the forest and nature filled me with anticipation.

I woke up early the next morning, while it was still dark outside. I had been an early riser ever since I was a kid; it was a habit I couldn't break even on a vacation! I whispered to Nina that I was going for a walk. She groggily waved to me and promptly went back to sleep. I quietly shut the door behind me and briskly walked out. I felt completely happy and alive as I stepped out into the chilly dawn. The landscape was dramatically different than the crowded city I chose to live in. The sweet smells of nature filled my senses. The sky was lightening and birds chirped noisily from nests concealed in trees. Thickets of wild and wondrously beautiful flowers peeped from between tall tree trunks.

I thrust my hands deep into my jacket and soaked in the beauty of the early morning. Breathing deeply, I urged myself to go faster on the narrow mountain lane as it wound its way up hugging the forest. Turning with the road, I noticed something glinting behind the bushes to my left. I took a few steps to get a closer look at the shiny object. What I saw took me by complete surprise. A rough wooden plaque was nailed to a tree with a brilliant golden star stuck to one corner. If it hadn't been for the shining piece of metal, I would have completely missed it. The plaque had a mystical quote carved beautifully in the wood. It read, *"When you open the gates of courage, fear walks out first."*

What could that mean? I stood amongst the bushes and puzzled over this mystery. Why would someone waste their wisdom in a desolate stretch like this? Who could it be? And what did the gold star stand for? Still bewildered, I looked around to see if I could spot anyone. A beautiful gate seemed to appear before me, leading to a house further inside! The green bamboo gate was so well camouflaged that it could easily be missed in the thick foliage.

I took a few tentative steps forward to check it out. As I stood debating the wisdom of letting curiosity and a misplaced sense of adventure outweigh common sense, there rose in the air an incredibly melodious song. A man was singing an ode to nature and its glory in the most beautiful manner I had ever heard sung. I felt a strange happiness and joy awaken in my heart.

The unseen singer paused once in a while to play his flute, making the musical rendition even more magical. I was surprised at my own reaction since I am wary of people who appear to be saints. I was helplessly attracted to this music which transcended any religious or spiritual experience I had had before. There was dedication and purity in the stranger's voice. I was drawn to this voice, and my feet tapped in rhythm. I couldn't help thinking that the Universe had given me a sign. Life has a way of taking us to the right place; we just have to look for the signs. Maybe, my job was not to question, but to simply follow my instincts.

I stepped inside the gate and crossed a shrub-lined path going up. The path ended abruptly, and I found myself in one of the most stunning gardens I had set my eyes on. It was landscaped in a large semi-circle and covered with velvety green grass. Several exotic and radiant flowers grew in lush bunches around the edges of the garden. The green contrasted brilliantly with the multicoloured flower-beds all around. I could make out several trees in the distance, laden with exotic fruit. Smack in the middle of this garden was another star, this time made of pebbles and embedded in the soft grass. Here it was again, that mysterious star shape! What was this person's connection to a star? As I looked up from this unbelievably beautiful sight, I was spellbound by a spectacular house rising from the base of this exotic garden.

The house was made of wood, and obviously handcrafted. It was clear that the person who had built it didn't much care for conventional symmetry that called for a perfection of lines. Planks of wood in different textures and hues jutted out at seemingly odd angles. The suspense was too much for me. There was no harm in saying hello. I knocked twice on the wooden door and stood back. The music stopped abruptly, and I imagined a very old person struggling to their feet, irritated at the unwelcome guest. The door was answered promptly, and I couldn't help being startled as it swung open. A man moved forward to reveal himself.

To my utter amazement, a young, tall, attractive, and obviously urban man stood framed in the doorway. He seemed to be in his early forties. His long, black hair was gathered into a short pony tail. Coupled with his faded blue jeans and pure white cotton kurta, he looked nothing short of a classy rock star. In his right hand he held a beautiful flute as he surveyed me. "So, I am not as well hidden as I had thought," he said grinning. His honest deep black eyes seemed full of mirth, as I noticed his obvious good health. He spoke in a rich baritone that matched his personality completely. "I am just kidding. Can I help you in any way?" he asked with sincerity.

I suddenly felt awkward about intruding on his privacy. "I am really sorry that I disturbed you. I was just passing by and saw the star. I guess my curiosity got the better of me," I said with an apologetic smile. The stranger looked at me keenly. "I have learned that life is meaningful only when we explore the possibilities. Who knows, I might prove to be your next good friend. Maybe, it is destined that we met. Please come in. My name is Jim," he offered with genuine warmth.

Who was this person? Where did he learn to talk like this? No one I had ever met for the first time, not to mention, in a jungle, had been this forthright with me. As we walked in, I looked in admiration at the neat insides of this unique house. The wooden house that seemed so rough and asymmetric from the outside was smooth and comfortable inside. We stood in a spacious living room with a huge glass window, from where I could see a beautiful pine forest sloping down, and the hills rising in the distance. What caught my attention, though, were several musical instruments leaning against the wooden walls of the living room. "So, you are a musician. I really enjoyed listening to you," I remarked. "Thanks! Music is a very important part of my life, though I make my living working as an architect. I designed and built the house you are standing in," he said, gesturing around us with his hand.

As far as I was concerned, the puzzle had just deepened. So, he wasn't some kind of a spiritual guru or a reclusive musician, but then, what was he doing here? Why was his house hidden? An architect needed to stay in the city to get work, instead of in a jungle, playing a flute! My thoughts were interrupted by his deep voice. "Care for a cup of tea, I was just about to make some for myself?" Jim asked. I thanked him. A cup of tea seemed like a great idea on a chilly morning.

As I sat down in his comfortable living room, I had an unmistakable feeling that this was not a chance meeting. There was a purpose to my being in Jim's house. At the risk of repeating myself, I believe the Universe has a plan for us. And it works only when we have a plan for ourselves. I had a lingering suspicion that Jim wasn't an ordinary person spending leisure time in the mountains. I knew a discovery awaited me and I had something to learn from this man. My recent surprise encounters had given me the courage to seek people from whom I could learn.

Jim returned with two steaming cups and sat opposite me. I knew this was my moment to ask him about the mystery of this place. "I am curious to know the meaning of the golden star and the quotation outside your gate. I haven't been able to get that mystical saying out of my mind. I love to learn something new, and you never know, it might be useful to me, as well," I said, hoping I didn't sound too weird. I was a student of life, and prayed that I had found yet another teacher in my journey. There were missing links in my understanding of how I could create a balanced and fulfilling life. Was Jim that teacher whom the Universe had chosen to help me this time?

Jim looked at me for a long moment. "The quotation you saw outside is of my own making. It is the biggest truth of my life," Jim said. I was still unclear about the truth of the quotation. "I recall exactly what is written outside. It says, 'When you open the gates of courage, fear walks out first.' How can courage and fear stay together in the first place?" I asked, genuinely confused at the contradiction.

Jim did not laugh at my simple question. "I completely understand your confusion. I lived with that belief for several years. What if I tell you a small story, and you can tell me what you understand by it," he offered. I agreed at once, and Jim told me an amazing story that deeply impacted me.

"When I was in high school, I already knew my parents expected me to become a doctor. I wasn't sure I wanted to become one, but didn't have the courage to say so." I wryly smiled as I recalled a familiar incident from my own life. "Before I knew, ten years of being a doctor had passed me by," Jim revealed. "You are a medical doctor by education?" I asked, astonished. "Frankly, there is a huge difference between being literate and being educated. I am literate enough to be a doctor, but am educated to be an artist who expresses himself through various art forms. It took me years to figure out this important difference. And I thank God every day for that. When we become that which we are not fit to be, our entire life goes out of alignment," Jim said serenely.

"How do you mean?" I asked, thinking back to my own life and the choices I had made. "This might sound strange to you, but the more I worked the less satisfied and happy I became. Now that I look back, it seems impossible how I pulled through a job I did not believe in. Though, I never fret about it, maybe that was life's way of nudging me towards my true calling. I had an absolutely clear vision of what I wanted to do once I quit medicine," Jim explained. I stared at him incredulously. "I don't know a doctor who quit being one!" I exclaimed.

Jim smiled. "I had the choice to continue being someone I did not believe in, or take a leap of faith and do what I truly loved. I chose the latter. It has been many blissful years of being who I really want to be. I am an architect, a musician, a gardener, and a painter. In fact, you must come by when I put up my painting exhibition in Mumbai next month," Jim offered with genuine excitement.

"Wow! Thanks, this is quite amazing. Know what, I just met a very prominent person who quit his career to start a vineyard," I said, almost to myself.

"There you go! You already got an example to understand what that quotation means," Jim said cheerfully. I looked at him for a second, and then realisation dawned on me. I had heard Kian's entire story, but until Jim gave me the right context, I had missed the profound learning. I had such happiness written all over my face that Jim began to laugh. "Do not take offence my friend. I am laughing because this is such a moment of joy. I guess this is very important to you," Jim said apologetically.

I looked at him happily. "You bet it is. Your quotation means that when we gather enough courage to move in the direction of our desires, then all our doubts and fears disappear. When we believe in ourselves the world follows us. When we unlock the gates of courage in our heart and mind, then no amount of discouraging thoughts can defeat us. We become free of our fears the moment we take a step forward to face them. Am I right about that?" I asked excitedly.

"You said it, mate! I don't think I could have put it better. Let me add to your understanding, and you will realise that the same principle applies to many things in life. Courage and fear are complimentary opposites of each other, like the yin and yang of life. They are seemingly contrary forces, but are interdependent and interconnected. It's like day and night, both cannot exist in the same place at the same time, but you cannot separate day from night or vice versa. When we harness the inherent will power of our mind and feel and act courageously, then fear will disappear. And if we feed our fear, then courage will leave us. This is nature's law. It is perfectly logical and beautifully designed by the Universe to help us lead a fulfilling life. Think about this. When we truly love someone, hatred cannot exist. When we genuinely forgive, there is no place for revenge. If our spirit is joyful we cannot be sad. When we believe in abundance, poverty will disappear. Positive always replaces the negative. We have to strongly desire to do so, that is the key. Anyone can do it," Jim declared with absolute confidence.

I must admit it was impossible not to be touched by Jim's enthusiasm. His spirit was infectious. I was floored by his ability to have explained what he did so simply. The laws that governed a fulfilling life were not complicated. They were easy to understand and implement. Wasn't this Maya's mantra, as well? Our past and present cannot happily live together. We can choose to exist in our past with our fear and regrets, or decide to live in our present with hope and faith.

I had already made changes in my lifestyle and relationships by using the same principle. The moment I had stopped being afraid of other people's disappointments with me in the past, I had gathered enough courage to make new beginnings with them in the present. Whether I understood it or not, the law had come into action. When I opened the gates of courage, fear had walked out first. Jim had been watching me keenly and noticed my unspoken excitement at all the rapid connections I was making about the wisdom I had gained. Truly, there is not a single new age problem that does not have a cure in age-old wisdom. We just have to be brave enough to discover the answers, and a transformed life awaits us at every step.

"I cannot tell you what it means for me to have understood this, Jim. I have been too busy competing and running hard for the last twenty-five years of my life. I know there is more to me as a person and a professional. I really hope I get there," I confessed.

"You have opened the gates of courage already, my friend. Just wait and watch how new options will come flooding into your life," Jim assured me. Suddenly, he paused and looked at me as if he had forgotten to say something. "I must share with you one last truth that I learned from one of my gurus," Jim said. "Let me explain it like this. You will agree that we are supreme beings on this planet?" Jim asked. I nodded in agreement. "We are superior not so much because of Darwin's evolutionary findings, but because of our ability to call our internal power to action at will," Jim revealed. "We are the only beings on earth that have the ability to choose to be anything we wish. In the same spirit, we can choose to stop being what we don't wish to be. We are divine because we have the ability to rise above our animal instincts and lead a spiritual existence in our physical form.

Not many people understand that life is expansive. Life is not just about our petty concerns and complaints. The game is bigger than that, much bigger. The playing field is enormous when it comes to personal success," Jim said animatedly. I had begun to understand where Jim was leading me. "As I pursue my own goals, I make every effort to meaningfully contribute to others' goals. If we help them get what they want, then we can easily achieve what we want. Have no doubt in your mind, my friend, that others are not just an important, but a necessary ingredient, to our success and peace. Making a difference to those around us is a natural expression of our higher purpose. Our prosperity is meant to make another's life beautiful. That is what is meant by – contribution," Jim said spiritedly.

I was impressed by Jim's simple yet beautiful philosophy. One thought had been nagging me and I decided to ask Jim about it. "Do we have to find our true calling in life before we can make a contribution to others? Can we serve our higher purpose even if we are stuck on the wrong path in life?"

"Excellent question, my friend," said Jim nodding wisely.

"It would be incorrect to assume that only a chosen few can serve their higher purpose in life. At the same time, wisdom is more logical than we believe it to be. When we live a life based on other people's expectations, we cause unhappiness to ourselves and to them. Our lack of contentment and joy puts every aspect of our life out of whack. Imagine making a contribution then? If we hardly have the desire to make ourselves happy, how can we make another happy? It might become an uphill task that saps our energy. It makes no sense. Our own cup should be overflowing with joy and abundance before others can take a sip from it.

"Through my own experience, I have noticed that when we fail to live out our dreams, we become insensitive to ourselves, as well as to others. Our nature turns callous and uncaring. Love is replaced by resentment and revenge towards those we hold responsible for our unfulfilled lives. That is why it is so important to follow our desire and find our true calling. Frankly, we are more afraid of our success than of our failure. We must give ourselves a second chance," Jim said taking a deep breath.

I pondered over Jim's startling revelations about life and its actual nature. I might have spent a lifetime seeking this knowledge in books, which I had so accidentally chanced upon in the midst of a forest. As always, I doubted if this was an accident after all. Too many kind and generous people had crossed my path in the last few months for me to believe that even for a moment.

"Wow! I cannot explain to you, Jim, how you have been able to provide the missing pieces of my life's jigsaw. I know I am at the brink of a major transformation, yet some answers had eluded me. I am deeply grateful to you," I said sincerely. Jim blushed a little at my frank praise, and simply inclined his head to acknowledge my heartfelt appreciation.

Our brief, yet enlightening session had come to an end, or at least, so I thought. I stood up and extended my right hand with much gratitude towards Jim. Ignoring my hand, Jim gave me a big smile, and put his arms around me in a warm hug. I smiled back and nodded at him. I knew I had made a good friend, just as he had predicted. As I was walking out of Jim's home, I suddenly remembered something important. "You haven't yet told me about the star. What does it mean?"

"Oh that," he shrugged with a smile. "That one is simple. The five arms of the star stand for a personal philosophy I maintain in my life. I call it my 'five star' philosophy," he said with a wink.

"It's a simple philosophy with five key points that I try to implement:

1. **Love** — To love myself first with all my faults and weaknesses, so I can love others with all of theirs.

2. **Forgive** — Make sure I genuinely forgive and let the past remain in the past, so I can love more abundantly and attract love into my own life.

3. **Rejuvenate** — Nurture an open mindset, a healthy body, and a happy spirit, so I can take my higher purpose as far as I am able to.

4. **Contribute** — Always remember to give as much to others as I expect to receive for myself, and know that I will take nothing with me when I die.

5. **Be Happy** — Make it my supreme purpose to live a happy and complete life, and give happiness to others. A life lived without joy is a life not lived.

"As far as the star in the middle of the garden is concerned, well, we can solve that mystery right away," said Jim, moving briskly towards the garden. He gestured to me to stand on the star embedded in the grass, and look up at the house. Following his cryptic instructions, I moved forward and did as he asked. As I looked up, I was stunned by an unbelievably beautiful sight. The seemingly haphazard planks that jutted out of the house at odd angles had come together in the shape of a star. Jim's house was the centre of the star, with five graceful arms pointing outward. The house had turned into a shining star as the rising sun glowed brilliantly from behind, bathing it in a golden halo.

As I walked back to our resort, I no longer felt chilly. My heart was filled with immense warmth and thankfulness. I felt confident that I had got a peek into the bright future that lay ahead. I went over the remarkable series of events and people that had brought me this far. I was no longer the same person. I had changed deep inside. I could never go back to my ineffective ways or to my unhealthy lifestyle. I now knew something that made me strong enough to change my life in fundamental ways. That first meeting with Maya seemed like a distant event. In fact I didn't identify with that person at all. Today was the first day of a fantastic future I had stepped into. I was fully prepared for both challenges and opportunities. I literally felt on top of the world! A fitting tribute to a mountain holiday !

CHAPTER 8

Message in the Mountains

Quotable Quote: When you open the gates of courage, fear walks out first.

5 Powerful Thoughts

➤ Life is meaningful only when we explore the possibilities of what we desire to do

➤ We are more afraid of our success than our failure. It is easier to fail than to make a focussed effort at super success.

➤ There is a huge difference between being literate and being educated. Our University degree does not dictate our life's mission.

➤ Life goes out of alignment when we pursue the wrong goals.

➤ The Universe has a plan for us when we have one for ourselves. Knowing what we want is the only way to get it.

The Master Key: Stepping forward to face our fears helps overcome them for the rest of our lives

Action Point

Make a list of your fears. Examine them logically, and address each of them in the best way you can. Then stop thinking about them. Keep checking if your deepest desires reflect in your most important work.

Lessons of Chapter Nine

 *Pain can be sorted out with love, understanding and patience*

 *Life is abundant and forgiving*

 *When we open the gates of courage, fear walks out first*

 *Life has a way of leading us to the right path*

CHAPTER 9

An Awakened Life

*"Trust in dreams, for in them is hidden
the gate to eternity."*

~Kahlil Gibran

I have shared my extraordinary story with you, and feel a sense of great joy. I do think that the painful parts of our lives can be sorted out with understanding, love, and patience. I don't under-estimate the value of others' help either. Maybe this book could act as your friend that can help you. Most importantly, I hope you will find the space and time in your busy life to implement what you read here. I will be deeply indebted if you will take these lessons and share them with those you love and care about. Who knows, you could start your own *'wisdom revolution'* !

I deeply wish for you to use these lessons on a daily basis. What we do everyday becomes a habit – both the good stuff and the bad. You can choose the good stuff starting today. It is not difficult at all. Don't let anyone mislead you on this one. Those who over-estimate the difficulty of turning life around haven't found the courage to accept that they can change their lives. Simple. Your journey can be smooth and fulfilling as well.

Life has a way of leading us to the right path. Yet many of us struggle needlessly by denying the truth that is staring us in the face. I know this, because I've done it in the past. From my own intimate experience, and after making several mistakes, I understand how we walk into traps. Sometimes we ignore the signals from our body until it breaks down and we fall seriously ill. At times we refuse to listen to our own good judgement, which results in painful mistakes at home and with others. We forget to nurture our joyful eternal spirit and create extreme unhappiness and depression for ourselves. Or, we ignore the principles of integrity and contribution, falling deeper into greed and insensitivity.

Here is the best part of the news, even when we wilfully end up on the wrong path, life doesn't stop giving us opportunities for transformation. Life is abundant and forgiving. We see it as harsh and unforgiving when we fail to stop in our busy lives and pay heed to its lessons. I was a weary traveller when I began my journey of transformation. Now that you have read my story, you will believe that I did not struggle painfully to receive the wisdom that I did. My teachers appeared when I needed them the most. Their words touched my heart and my life in unimaginable ways. I learnt from them when I was at my worst, so there is no proof to say that once we make mistakes life does not give us a chance. The most important thing is to give ourselves a chance. Leave the past where it belongs, in the past. Life then beautifully falls into place.

I don't under-estimate my own inner voice, or the silent work of my eternal spirit which guided me in using my new-found wisdom in the best possible way. We can improve our lives instantly by listening to the good judgement and common sense we all possess. As I said in the beginning of my story, we don't need extraordinary circumstances or people to enlighten us. We are all enlightened. The Universe made it so. Our hard work lies in listening to our inner voice, and to life's signals, that always show us the right path. I have discovered that when we do this, we begin to think wisely, and wonderful actions follow from this. That is enlightenment. Not difficult, in fact much easier than you can imagine.

I hope the extraordinary journey of an ordinary man like me has made you think of your own journey. Let me now share with you a decision I took to change my life for the rest of my life. After a year of bringing remarkable changes at work with the help of my team, I decided to take one of the biggest decisions of my life. I quit as the chief executive officer of one of India's most prestigious and prosperous IT companies. When I resigned from my job, I felt truly 'unemployed' after decades. Must admit it was a wonderful feeling! You might want to ask if it was tough to let go of my life's identity and hard work? Believe it or not, quitting my job was one of the easiest decisions of my life. It made me smile and my heart felt lighter as I handed over my resignation. Two weeks ago, I walked out of my office, never to go back to a corporate job again. Not because it was not worthy, but I had realised it was not my calling. I had other ambitions to follow, other paths to explore. And I can't wait to begin a new phase in my professional life.

After much thinking, I concluded that no job is good or bad by itself. Rather, the way we handle our work and lifestyle, while we do our job, makes it healthy or unhealthy. I now know that to make life successful in a hectic job we need solid judgement to differentiate between greed and need, want and desire, enough and excess, dedication and addiction, purpose and obsession, contentment and complacency, and working hard and slogging. The super-busy life we lead every single day clouds our judgement, making it difficult to sort through these important distinctions. Without pausing and thinking, we are sure to fall into a trap that can ruin our good health and family life. I truly hope that sharing my ups and downs with you will help you analyse your own situation better.

Nina and I have taken a sabbatical together to reassess the goals and purpose of our life. We are currently on a tour of Europe, where we are meeting some friends and having a great time living every single day. This is also precious time for us to think through our life ahead. But then, all of that will take another book!

I cannot guarantee that my future will turn out to be as successful as my corporate career. Who knows, it might turn out to be much more spectacular and fulfilling than I have imagined. I believe with all my heart that the Universe has bigger plans for me and for you. Remember, the Universe is listening to your every thought. What are you asking of it today? I hope you are prepared to dream BIG! May you find your true calling and lead a long and magnificent life. This is my wish for you.

CHAPTER 9

An Awakened Life

Quotable Quote: Our hard work lies in listening to our inner voice.

5 Powerful Thoughts

➤ Pain – our own and others' – can be sorted out with understanding, love, and patience

➤ The way we handle our work makes it healthy or unhealthy. The key lies in our approach rather than in our job description.

➤ The Universe has bigger plans for me and for you. Believe in it.

➤ Life is abundant and forgiving. There is room for tremendous success in the dimmest of situations.

➤ We all have enough good judgement and common sense to lead a great life.

The Master Key: Life has a way of leading us to the right path, if we keep reading the signs

Action Point

Give yourself a second chance and be confident that a far more profitable path will open for you. Trust your heart to lead you to your true calling in life. Work that resonates with your deepest beliefs brings the most success !

RESOURCES

The 'Personal Breakthrough' Work Sheet

Answer these ten golden questions that encompass your personal and professional life. Helpful examples are given below each question. Discuss your responses with someone you trust. Implement your answers over the next 30 days. You must ensure that you live your answers.

1. **What do I value deeply and sincerely as a person?**
    Example: Integrity

    ....

    ....

2. **What are the top three objectives of my personal life?**
    Example: To do what I believe in

    i)...

    ii)..

    iii)...

3. **What are my deepest values as a professional?**
    Example: Teamwork

    ....

    ....

4. **What are the top three objectives of my professional life?**
    Example: To approach my work in a healthy way

    i)..

    ii)..

    iii)..

5. **Which are the three most destructive work habits I have? What am I going to do to get rid of them in the next thirty days?**
    Example: I smoke when I am stressed out. I will believe that I am strong enough to resist.

    i)..

    ii)..

    iii)..

6. **What actions am I ready to take to nurture my physical, mental, and emotional health?**

    Physical.
    Example: Walk one km daily

    ....

    Mental.
    Example: Read a good book

    ....

    Emotional.
    Example: Express my feelings when necessary

    ....

7. **What key steps am I willing to take to nurture my personal and family life?**

   Personal.

   Example: Give importance to my desires and plans

   ....

   ....

   Family.

   Example: Balance relationships with personal goals

   ....

   ....

8. **Which key roles am I most capable of handling at my workplace? Am I investing my energy in excelling at these roles?**

   Example: Vice President/Project head

   ....

   ....

   ....

9. **What two steps will I take to develop leaders in my team?**

   Example: Hear people out when they make a suggestion

   i)..

   ii)..

10. **If I quit my job today, what are the top two professional options that I have?**

    Example: Invest in higher studies

    i)..

    ii)..

Your Personal Five Star Philosophy

Read all the five arms of the Five Star Philosophy. Set aside a quiet time and think deeply about each of them in relation to your personal life. Then fill in your thoughts against each of the five questions.

LOVE

Who are the people I love deeply? What can I do every day to make sure they know I love them? Do I love myself completely?

....

....

....

FORGIVE

Have I forgiven those who have wronged me? Have I forgiven myself? Do I think more about my past or my present?

....

....

....

REJUVENATE

Do I have an open mindset that allows for fresh thinking? Which activities make me feel the most enthusiastic? Are my body and spirit keeping up with my ambitions?

....

....

....

CONTRIBUTE

Do I consider myself a generous person? Whom have I contributed to in the last week? Do I understand that I need to give in order to receive?

....

....

....

BE HAPPY

Are my inner spirit and mind happy? Do I look for happiness inside or expect others to make me happy? Have I made anyone happy today? Is my life joyful in my own estimation?

....

....

....

ABOUT LEADERSHIP SUCCESS SOLUTIONS

Shaping the young to lead the future

Leadership Success Solutions is a unique training and consulting organisation. While leadership is usually targeted to a corporate audience, we primarily focus on designing and conducting leadership workshops for school and college students. The youth today are very well informed, and have many more options to choose from, than in the past. We believe that leadership will be the key differentiator for young people to balance personal and professional success in the future. Our workshops are designed to give them this edge, and also provide them with some important life-skills. Our facilitators use their experiences from the corporate world to train the youth, and equip them with real world knowledge and expertise to face tough challenges. Our workshops are fun-filled, while allowing each participant to tap into their leadership potential, through group and individual exercises.

We conduct programs on the following key areas:

- Leadership
- Communication
- Self-motivation
- Team building

For more information on training solutions:
Website: www.leadershipsuccesssolutions.com
Email: training@leadershipsuccesssolutions.com

To engage Sonali for a key-note address:
Email: sonali@leadershipsuccesssolutions.com

CONNECT WITH SONALI ON THE WEB:

FACEBOOK: Join the Corporate Nirvana Facebook page to share your thoughts and read regular updates from Sonali

TWITTER: Tweet her @sonalidsilva for inspiring quotes and useful tips on leadership

BLOG: Follow her motivating and informative blogs at http://sonalidsilva.blogspot.com/

WEBSITE: Log on to the www.leadershipsuccesssolutions.com to know more about Sonali and her work

AUTHOR PROFILE

Sonali Masih-D'silva

Sonali Masih-D'silva is the co-founder of Leadership Success Solutions. Her forte lies in translating leadership principles into action. Over the last fifteen years, she has trained more than ten thousand participants on various topics of self-development. She has conducted workshops across US, UK, and Europe as well. Her training style can be best described as fun, engaging, and positive, and has won her much appreciation.

Sonali is passionate about self-development, and began her career at twenty-one, teaching professional skills to college students, older than her at the time. She then did her MBA in Human Resources, and found her first job with the Indian Institute of Management (IIM), Indore, as an academic associate in organisational behaviour. A year later, she embarked on a formal consulting career. Over the next three years, she trained for several leading public and private sector companies. Sonali eventually joined Wipro Ltd., as an in-house behavioural training consultant. An association of six years followed that helped her not just learn a lot, but make some life-long friends, as well. Here, she also earned several prestigious international certifications in behavioural methodology, curriculum, and psychometrics.

Sonali has invested a major part of her life helping people to be their best. She encourages her participants to dream big and cultivate courage. Her belief is that our circumstances can delay us, but not stop us. This has led to accomplishments that seemed impossible when she began.

Corporate Nirvana is her first attempt at writing fiction to convey what she strongly believes in. Her articles on leadership and management themes are published regularly.

Besides training, Sonali loves to read books, and is always excited to add a new one to her bookshelf. Her spare time is also spent in indulging in her love for art and painting.

Sonali lives with her husband, and they spend their time between Delhi and Mumbai for work.